The UK Air Fryer Cookbook for Beginners

Simple & Affordable Air Fryer Recipes Everyday For Your Family and Friends incl. Side Dishes, Special Desserts and More

Doris E. Oropeza

Copyright© 2022 By Doris E.Oropeza All Rights Reserved

This book is copyright protected. It is only for personal use. You cannot amend, distribute, sell, use, quote or paraphrase any part of the content within this book, without the consent of the author or publisher.

Under no circumstances will any blame or legal responsibility be held against the publisher, or author, for any damages, reparation, or monetary loss due to the information contained within this book, either directly or indirectly.

Disclaimer Notice:

Please note the information contained within this document is for educational and entertainment purposes only. All effort has been executed to present accurate, up to date, reliable, complete information. No warranties of any kind are declared or implied. Readers acknowledge that the author is not engaged in the rendering of legal, financial, medical or professional advice. The content within this book has been derived from various sources. Please consult a licensed professional before attempting any techniques outlined in this book.

By reading this document, the reader agrees that under no circumstances is the author responsible for any losses, direct or indirect, that are incurred as a result of the use of the information contained within this document, including, but not limited to, errors, omissions, or inaccuracies.

Contents

INTRODUCTION 1
What's the Air Fryer? 2
Choosing the Right Air Fryer for You.. 3
What to Cook vs Foods to Avoid in the Air Fryer 5
Guide to Cleaning & Maintenance 8
Care Tips for Your Air Fryer 9
Air Fryer Frequently Asked Questions 10

Chapter 1 Breakfasts 12
Sausage and Egg Breakfast Burrito 12
Portobello Eggs Benedict 12
Broccoli-Mushroom Frittata 13
Poached Eggs on Whole Grain Avocado Toast 13
Cheddar Eggs 13
Golden Avocado Tempura 14
Parmesan Ranch Risotto 14
Spinach Omelet 14
Buffalo Egg Cups 15
Tomato and Cheddar Rolls 15
Sausage and Cheese Balls 16
Bourbon Vanilla French Toast.. 16
Cajun Breakfast Sausage... 16
Gluten-Free Granola Cereal 17
Western Frittata 17
Jalapeño and Bacon Breakfast Pizza 17

Honey-Apricot Granola with Greek Yoghurt 18
Banana-Nut Muffins 18
French Toast Sticks 19
Oat Bran Muffins 19

Chapter 2 Fast and Easy Everyday Favourites 20

Spinach and Carrot Balls 20
Beery and Crunchy Onion Rings 20
Simple Pea Delight 20
Air Fried Courgette Sticks 21
Bacon Pinwheels 21
Air Fried Shishito Peppers 21
Beetroot Salad with Lemon Vinaigrette 22
Herb-Roasted Veggies 22
Simple and Easy Croutons 22
Corn Fritters 23
Easy Devils on Horseback 23
Peppery Brown Rice Fritters 23
Rosemary and Orange Roasted Chickpeas 24
Easy Roasted Asparagus 24

Chapter 3 Poultry 25

Buttermilk-Fried Drumsticks 25
Sriracha-Honey Chicken Nuggets 25
Buffalo Chicken Cheese Sticks 26
Turkey Meatloaf 26
Italian Crispy Chicken 26
Crisp Paprika Chicken Drumsticks 27
Lettuce-Wrapped Turkey and Mushroom Meatballs 28
Jalapeño Popper Hasselback Chicken 28
Herbed Roast Chicken Breast 29

Chicken Croquettes with Creole Sauce 29

Gochujang Chicken Wings 30

Piri-Piri Chicken Thighs 30

Nacho Chicken Fries 31

Cajun-Breaded Chicken Bites.. 31

Lemon Thyme Roasted Chicken.. 32

Chapter 4 Beef, Pork, and Lamb.. 33

Cantonese BBQ Pork 33

Bacon-Wrapped Pork Tenderloin 33

Cheese Crusted Chops 34

Kale and Beef Omelet.. 34

Vietnamese Grilled Pork 34

Sirloin Steak with Honey-Mustard Butter 35

Lamb Burger with Feta and Olives.. 35

Short Ribs with Chimichurri 36

Italian Sausage Links 36

Minute Steak Roll-Ups 37

Herb-Crusted Lamb Chops 37

Garlic Butter Steak Bites 38

Kheema Meatloaf 38

Filipino Crispy Pork Belly 38

Apple Cornbread Stuffed Pork Loin 39

Bulgogi Burgers 40

Fajita Meatball Lettuce Wraps 41

Barbecue Ribs... 41

Ritzy Skirt Steak Fajitas 42

Caraway Crusted Beef Steaks.. 42

Pork Milanese 43

Pork Schnitzels with Sour Cream and Dill Sauce 43

Sausage-Stuffed Peppers 44

Sausage and Cauliflower Arancini 44

Herbed Lamb Steaks 45

Chicken Fried Steak with Cream Gravy 46

Parmesan-Crusted Pork Chops 46

Bo Luc Lac 47

Kielbasa and Cabbage 47

Bacon and Cheese Stuffed Pork Chops 48

Chapter 5 Fish and Seafood 49

Stuffed Sole Florentine 49

Friday Night Fish-Fry 49

Salmon with Fennel and Carrot 50

Mackerel with Spinach 50

Garlic Butter Prawns Scampi 50

Honey-Balsamic Salmon 51

Air Fried Crab Bun 51

Oregano Tilapia Fingers 51

Salmon on Bed of Fennel and Carrot 52

Rainbow Salmon Kebabs 52

Prawn Kebabs 52

Smoky Prawns and Chorizo Tapas 53

Swordfish Skewers with Caponata 53

Crab Cakes with Sriracha Mayonnaise 54

Parmesan-Crusted Halibut Fillets 55

Mediterranean-Style Cod 55

Simple Buttery Cod 55

Classic Prawns Empanadas 56

Lemony Prawns 56

Crustless Prawn Quiche 56

Chapter 6 Vegetables and Sides ... 58

Garlic-Parmesan Crispy Baby Potatoes ... 58

Lebanese Baba Ghanoush ... 58

Parmesan-Thyme Butternut Squash ... 58

Fried Brussels Sprouts ... 59

Fried Courgette Salad ... 59

Spicy Roasted Bok Choy ... 60

Marinara Pepperoni Mushroom Pizza ... 60

Fig, Chickpea, and Rocket Salad ... 60

Herbed Shiitake Mushrooms ... 61

Dijon Roast Cabbage ... 61

Potato with Creamy Cheese ... 61

Buttery Green Beans ... 62

Roasted Grape Tomatoes and Asparagus ... 62

Mexican Corn in a Cup ... 62

Courgette Fritters ... 63

Lemon-Thyme Asparagus ... 63

Five-Spice Roasted Sweet Potatoes ... 63

Spiced Honey-Walnut Carrots ... 64

Broccoli Tots ... 64

Garlic and Thyme Tomatoes ... 64

Chapter 7 Fast and Easy Everyday Favourites ... 65

Air Fried Broccoli ... 65

Cheesy Potato Patties ... 65

Beef Bratwursts ... 65

Baked Chorizo Scotch Eggs ... 65

Crunchy Fried Okra ... 66

Buttery Sweet Potatoes ... 66

Indian-Style Sweet Potato Fries ... 67

Purple Potato Chips with Rosemary 67
Scalloped Veggie Mix 67
Cheesy Baked Grits 68
Traditional Queso Fundido 68
Cheesy Chilli Toast 68
Baked Cheese Sandwich 69
Baked Halloumi with Greek Salsa 69
Air Fried Butternut Squash with Chopped Hazelnuts 69
Air Fried Tortilla Chips 70
Cheesy Jalapeño Cornbread 70

Chapter 8 Desserts 71
Pineapple Wontons 71
Cream Cheese Danish 71
Almond Shortbread 72
Crustless Peanut Butter Cheesecake 72
Blackberry Peach Cobbler with Vanilla 72
Pecan and Cherry Stuffed Apples 73
Pecan Brownies 73
Baked Brazilian Pineapple 74
Cardamom Custard 74
Fried Cheesecake Bites 74
Chocolate and Rum Cupcakes 75
Tortilla Fried Hand Pies 75
Eggless Farina Cake 76
White Chocolate Cookies 76
Apple Wedges with Apricots 77

INTRODUCTION

Using an Air Fryer helped me lose more than 30kgs.

You see, I've been a fat kid my whole life. I remember the day my mom sent me to school with a bag full of fresh fruits and vegetables for lunch. "Please, Rosie. Just this once," she pleaded. I took the produce grudgingly, in a sense of defeat. I didn't want to be healthier and more productive, that wasn't my problem. My problem was how much I weighed; not what I ate.

It was like she forgot that my classmates knew me as the fat kid. And then I got to school and everyone laughed at me. They made fun of my chubby cheeks and my big, silly smile. No one wanted to trade with me or sit with me or even walk to the front of the lunch line.

I was embarrassed. To this day, I can still see the tears that silently welled up in my eyes. "There's Rosie," they'd whisper, their voices dripping with disdain.

At that age, I had no idea how to handle my plight. I started eating my carrots and celery on the playground, which only made me feel more isolated. I just couldn't seem to win. And when I got home that night, my mom told me she had found a magic fix for me, some special weight loss program. I was to eat less, no more than 130 pounds. "It's the only way you'll ever lose the weight," she said. In short, I was being pimped out as a guinea pig. Of course, my mom didn't realize that. I just felt like she didn't love me anymore—she loved my fat-free future instead.

The problem is, I couldn't keep up. I didn't have enough energy to exercise, so I continued eating for hours and hours on end. My weight continued to climb.

Then once I hit my teens, it became too much for me to bear. I was angry at everyone and everything. I felt like I had no control over my life, and it was all because of the extra baggage. I had tried everything, and the only thing that worked was making me feel sick and unhappy.

Everyone's body is different, and that's true. I guess for me, eating less food just made me feel unsatisfied. And as a result of my hunger, I ate still more. No one could stop me.

And I turned my anger inward, blaming myself for being unsafe. Why didn't I have any self-control? Why couldn't I just eat normally?

But then, in 2013, the tables turned. Mom and I were at a grocery store when we came across this newfangled contraption called an air fryer. The box had a picture of a nice golden-brown drumstick and the words "MORE TASTY, LESS FAT!"

"What does that mean?" Mom asked. "Well, I'm guessing we're going to find out," I said. We read through and it said that you could fry chicken without using oil. Now, Mom and I both felt confused.

"We don't fry chicken without oil," Mom said. "Why would we do that?" I just shrugged my shoulders, but to me, it seemed like a pretty good idea. Mom suggested that we buy the biggest one they had. I happily paid for it, received it at home, and brought it to my room. I eagerly unpacked the box and found a recipe book. "I can't wait to cook breakfast in this baby!" I told Mom. I pulled off the plastic wrapping and put it on a shelf. That night, I cooked dinner in the air fryer.

I admit, at first I wasn't entirely convinced that it would work. But after I watched the drumstick come out crispy and golden, I was surprised. "Amazing," I said. "I can't believe it." I could feel myself getting excited about trying new foods in a whole new way. After all, the concept was pretty simple: food goes in the basket, and a lid is placed on top. The air fryer heats up and cooks the food slowly. It's as easy as that. No oil is required and you won't have to burn yourself with a frying pan, either.

But the best news, perhaps, is that air fryers can help you lose weight. They preserve all the flavor and integrity of food while reducing your fat intake and calorie count. You still get to have the taste and texture that you love, but without all the greasy calories.

So if you are new to Air Fryers, keep reading. In the next few pages, I'll share with you a little about air fryers, how to make the right choice, and tips to use, maximize, and maintain your air fryer. I will also answer some frequently asked questions about Air fryers.

And who knows? Maybe even you can do it too.

What's the Air Fryer?

What started out as a small kitchen gadget company has now become one of the fastest-growing companies in Europe. A couple of years ago, if you had mentioned the word 'air fryer' no one would understand what you were talking about, but now, if you don't have one, you're seen as being out of the loop. Don't worry though, you're not alone! Many people out there do not understand what this powerful kitchen gadget really is.

There is a very satisfying answer to the question 'What is an Air Fryer?' and it's not complicated, actually: It's a machine that uses hot air to fry food. Yes, that's it! The food is placed in a basket, or on a tray or rack inside and hot air is forced around the food to cook it. The word 'fry' is a bit misleading, as this is not deep frying, even though the food does get cooked in oil. However, the oil has to be very light and drips out as it cooks, leaving a much healthier option than deep frying.

A lot of people still think that air fryers are just a gimmick that can't actually cook food. That couldn't be further from the truth! This kitchen appliance is just as innovative on the inside as it is on the outside. The premise behind the air fryer is quite basic. It has a heat source and vent that allows hot air to circulate through the inside of the machine while food cooks in short bursts of time. In fact, chefs from all over the world can attest that cooking food in this way can be compared with professional cooking methods.

The air fryer is equipped with a thermostat that monitors the temperature inside the cooking chamber. The thermostat's main function is to regulate the flow and distribution of hot air around the food inside. This provides real cooking results within a short amount of time. The beauty of these machines is that they are versatile. You can fry, bake, roast, and even grill foods with them.

Some models are equipped with a removable rack that allows you to cook food in different ways. For instance, you can set the air fryer to bake and fill the inside with water to make it into a roasting oven. The model that I have installed at my house is actually three-in-one. It has a baking tray, roasting rack, and air fryer basket that allows me to cook all kinds of foods in the same machine!

Now we're moving on to the actual operation of an air fryer. The best thing about it is that it can be used by anyone. You don't need any special cooking skills or any particular experience to use one of these machines. All you need to do is plug it in, set the appropriate temperature and cook time, place your food inside, close the door and wait for the food to cook. That's all there is to it! You can eat in style without compromising on flavor or nutrition.

I will discuss the benefits of an air fryer in more details later, but for now, let's just say that it enhances the natural flavors of your food without making them too overbearing.

Choosing the Right Air Fryer for You

Navigating the sea of Air Fryers available on the market can be tough – there are many available in different sizes and with varying features. Some have preset cooking temperatures, while others can even cook food to a specified target level of doneness. It's worthwhile to make a list of needs and wants before deciding on which Air Fryer is right for you. Use this buying guide to help you choose the best air fryer for your needs and budget.

First, think about your needs. All air fryers are, at the end of the day, very similar and purpose-built. In this guide we'll give you some tips on how to buy an air fryer, then can help you decide which one is the best fit for you.

1. Your budget.

The price of an air fryer can vary dramatically, depending on the brand and features. Some are very affordable, while others are meant for commercial use. As a general rule of thumb, the more expensive models will have more features and settings to choose from. Whether these are worth the extra money is up to you, but my buying guide will help you make an informed decision on what you get for your money.

A cheap air fryer may be as good as the expensive one when it comes to cooking. However, more expensive models will more likely be built to last and have features that you can't find in a cheap one. With this in mind, feel free to spend a bit more on the better model.

2. Capacity and Size

There's no doubt that you'll want to get the biggest air fryer possible. The more baskets you can fit, the more food you can cook at once and the faster your air fryer will be. On top of that, it will save you money in terms of electricity because a small appliance requires less power than a large one (let's call it the Law of Energy Conservation).

It's worth noting, however, that some models come with a basket holder so that you don't have to buy them separately. If you can afford it and want the best performance out of your air fryer, then you'll want to invest in an appliance that has several baskets.

With regards to size, you'll need to make sure that your air fryer will fit in the place where you plan on using it. It should be big enough to accommodate the amount of food you want to cook but not so big that it takes an entire corner of your kitchen.

3. Ease of Use and Design

This is one of the areas where air fryers can score a lot of points. While some models take a lot of time and effort to use, others are really straightforward. They're quite simple to use, in fact; most modern air fryers have extremely clear instructions on how to cook healthy meals.

Models such as the Philips Airfryers use preprogrammed settings that do all the work for you. While these features may be convenient for some, others will prefer a more hands-on approach and personal choice over preset options. Unfortunately, there is no single product that is perfect in every category. It's up to you to decide what you need more

It's also smart to look at the famous user reviews online; there are plenty of people in the world who have used small air fryers for years, so their experiences should be informative. These people often share tips and tricks which can help you make healthy meals that you'll love.

4. Temperature Control

How Can You Cook Healthy Foods In The Air Fryer? An air fryer has to deal with a lot of problems in order to be able to cook food safely and efficiently. This is why there are several different types of air fryers available. The most basic type is the countertop model. These usually have no temperature control, although there are some exceptions.

If you ever want to cook something delicious and healthy in your air fryer, like fried chicken, for example, you'll need a model that can heat up to 175° or more. You'll also need an air fryer with enough power to deal with the massive amount of oil and fat from the chicken

5. Safety Features

Safety is an important consideration in all appliances, but especially so in something that heats food. Air fryers are safe, at least as safe as any other cooking appliance, but some models have added safety features that can be nice if you have little kids running around the house. For example, many models have an inbuilt temperature sensor that can alert you when unsafe cooking temperatures are reached. Some models have also come with safety features such as a shatterproof glass lid and tempered glass interior. It's also worth noting that some air fryers have interlocking lids, which means you can't stack more than two fryers on top of each other. This is great for storage but might not be the most convenient design.

6. Accessories and other benefits

Different models have different features that are unique to their own brand. Accessories such as the Philips Airfryer Attachment Kit includes a divider dish, 8-inch fry basket and two oil containers that allow you to cook two batches of food at once. Other brands come with various accessories such as the FoodSaver TurboSteam Air Fryer. These models will set you back more, but the extra accessories may prove highly useful.

Other brands, such as the GoWISE Air Fryer, include a recipe book or an online access to a recipe book. This is particularly handy for novice cooks looking to use their air fryers from day one.

7. Heat Distribution

One of the main advantages of an air fryer is its ability to cook food without a lot of oil. This is good news if you want to make healthier meals and cut down on fat, but it comes at a cost: the air fryer has to work really hard to deal with such a dry form of food.

If you're not careful and don't pick the right model, your food can easily become overcooked. When fat and oil are removed from food, the food begins to dehydrate. The result is a product that's dried out, shrunken, and will eventually be inedible.

The best way to prevent this problem is to choose an air fryer with a digital readout to indicate the level of heat inside the device. A digital readout is also advantageous because it's easy to use and will allow you to monitor the food without opening the air fryer.

What to Cook vs Foods to Avoid in the Air Fryer

Every beginner to an Air Fryer has the same burning question, what CAN I COOK in this thing? The truth is, you can fry just about anything in an air fryer. I have compiled a dozen of some of the BEST Air Fryer options you can make as a beginner, so stop worrying. Also, in order to make sure you're not going to accidentally burn your house down with an improperly prepared dish, I have compiled a list of five foods NOT TO COOK IN AN AIR FRYER.

Foods You Can Cook In An Air Fryer
1. Potato Chips
The best and easiest way to make crispy potato chips is in an air fryer. You can't really mess them up, but if you overcook them, watch out! It's not uncommon for home air fryers to have overheating problems and burn problems. My advice is to keep an eye on your chips and stop cooking when you are pleased with the results.

2. Chicken
Chicken is very easy to cook in an air fryer. Remove the skin from chicken prior to cooking, and do not cook with any marinades or breading. Many recipes and chicken wings on the market today are VERY greasy, which we all know can be dangerous for your health.

3. French Fries
French fries are always a good crispy treat when you have friends over or need something to eat when you're too lazy to cook an actual meal. French fries make a great snack in an air fryer, but make sure you're cooking them at just the right temperature so they are not burned. This can be tricky and frustrating to master, but with practice you will be able to successively cook perfect French Fries.

4. Fried Rice / Fried Rice Bowls / Fried Risotto / Fried Spaghetti
There is no way around it, fried rice is a special kind of food that requires some serious attention and patience when cooking. It's not the best thing to cook in an air fryer, but if you are adventurous and want to give it a shot, go for it. You will most definitely have a learning curve when making fried rice, but after a few attempts you should be able to create something spectacular.

5. Prawn/Crab
Lightly coat your prawn/crab before cooking to prevent them from sticking to the air fryer basket. Also, you might want to consider freezing them before air frying them. This will make sure they stay juicy and delicious.

6. Donuts / Doughnuts
Donuts and doughnuts can be a great treat in an air fryer. If you are going to cook them, make

sure you have a good glaze or icing to go along with it. I recommend a honey glaze, but this is always up for debate.

7. Eggs

Eggs are extremely easy to cook in an air fryer. Whether you want them hard boiled, soft boiled or scrambled, it's not going to affect the taste whatsoever. Just make sure you grease your air fryer basket so they don't stick together and burn. You can also try scrambling them with a little bit of cheese or spinach, which will add another layer of flavor.

8. Grilled Cheese

I know, I know… it's always been a question of IF you can air fry a grilled cheese. Well, I've done the research for you and found out you can… so go for it! Just try not to overcook or burn your sandwich pieces.

9. Chinese Food / Japanese Food / Thai Food / Indian Food

These foods are probably going to be the most difficult ones to master in an air fryer. If you're brave enough to cook some of these delicacies in your air fryer, you can use parchment paper or a cooking bag to keep them from making a big mess and falling apart. Also, grease your basket with olive oil or butter before placing any of these foods inside.

10. Chocolate Cake

Don't even think about cooking a chocolate cake in an air fryer, trust me on this one. If you want to try, you could always use chocolate icing or vegan icing, but I recommend trying a different recipe instead.

Foods To Avoid In An Air Fryer

1. Popcorn

Let's face it… popcorn is a very difficult food to make properly in an air fryer. It's not going to taste delicious and it most likely will stick to the basket, making a huge mess. Since you are just starting out, you should probably put off air frying popcorn for a later time.

2. Hamburgers (Mostly beef)

They're probably not going to taste great, and you most likely will have a big mess on your hands. Don't be discouraged though! Just keep working on learning how to air fry them the right way, and soon enough you will be able to master it.

3. Vegetables

Yes, you can cook vegetables in an air fryer, but using an air fryer to cook vegetables is a bit of a waste. With all the veggies, you will have to stick your hands in the basket and take them out multiple times during the cooking process. It's best to just use your oven or stovetop to steam or roast your veggies instead.

4. Fish

Fish are not as difficult to cook in an air fryer as chicken wings, but they can still cause some issues. The biggest problem is that fish can be very flimsy, so it tends to break apart when you try to grab the pieces and remove it from the basket. If you are a beginner and want to try fish in air fryer for the first time, I recommend sticking with lighter fish like tilapia or snapper, which won't break down as easily.

5. Noodles

In an air fryer, noodles will easily stick together in the basket. They will also burn very quickly because they require more attention than normal foods because they cook so quickly, which can make things very sticky and messy.

With that, I hope you know some of the easy recipes to start with, as well as a few you should stay away from. If you have any comments or questions, feel free to leave them in the comment section.

People all over the world are learning how to cook healthier in a more sustainable way. One way that is becoming increasingly popular is using an air fryer. If you want to know what the advantages of using an air fryer are, this section outlines some of the best ones out there.

1. No More Fat

One of the advantages of using an air fryer is that it lets you control what you're frying. This is something that you can't do if you're using a traditional oven to cook with oil. The heat is spread out so it doesn't build up, and that means you won't have as much fat getting into your food as if you were using oil. Instead, all of the fats are going right through to the bottom of your food, where the use of a air fryer pulls it out. This means you don't have to worry about things being greasy or soggy.

2. Cooks Quickly

One of the biggest disadvantages of other cooking methods is that you need to wait for your food to cook thoroughly before it's safe to eat. This can take hours in some cases, and the worst part is that your food is still raw until it's done cooking. With an air fryer, you get a nice crispy texture to your food while cutting down on the cooking time by more than half. No matter what you're cooking, you can have it done in far less time than ever before.

3. Easier to Clean

Many traditional ovens have a hard time getting the inside of them cleaned off and looking good again. When you use an air fryer, however, most of the mess stays on the outside because there is so much more space for it to be trapped in. This means that you don't have to worry about any food breaking loose and making a mess in your kitchen. All you need to do is wipe things off and get them cleaned up, and your kitchen will look better than ever before.

4. You Can Cook Multiple Things

One of the major advantages of an air fryer is that you can cook multiple things at once. This makes it easier for you to get meals ready for people if you're trying to feed a large number of people in a hurry. It also helps you to get things ready for a party so that you don't have to spend a lot of time in the kitchen to do it.

5. Easy to Use

Learning how to use an air fryer is very easy, and it can take just a matter of minutes. Most of them are going to come with instructions that will give you everything you need to know about them, and there are even videos online that show you exactly how they work. No matter what kind of air fryer you get, it's going to be easy to set up and start using right away.

6. Gets Hot Without Burning

While traditional frying will make your food as hot as the oil is sitting in, an air fryer gets hot all around so that you're cooking from all sides rather than just from the top and bottom. This means that your food is going to be much hotter without burning because the temperature is distributed evenly throughout the machine.

7. Has Locking Lid

One of the biggest problems that can come with using traditional ovens is that they don't have any kind of locking mechanism on them. This means that if you open them up, hot oil can spill out and burn you or your child. With an air fryer, however, the lid has a locking system built right into it so that it won't pop open by accident.

8. Energy Efficient

There's no question that using an air fryer is going to save you money on your energy bills over time because it uses far less electricity than traditional oven cooking. This means that you don't have to worry about it being expensive to operate, and you'll be able to keep the same cost of cooking without feeling like it's going to take a big bite out of your budget each month.

9. Has Temperature Controls

With an air fryer, you get to set the temperature controls so that you're getting exactly what you want out of your food. This is something that can't be done with traditional cooking, and it's a big benefit if you want to get the texture of your food just right. Instead of the food being soaked in oil or burning on the bottom, it's going to come out nice and crispy without either problem.

The best part is that it cooks your food with a uniform temperature so that it doesn't end up with hot spots or cold spots. This is one of the biggest problems with traditional cooking, and it makes things like cookies and potatoes harder to cook because they end up burning in certain spots. Instead, everything you cook will be heated evenly so that nothing goes to waste.

10. Can Be Used in Different Ways

There are some air fryers out there that can do more than just cook your food. Instead, they have baking systems integrated into them as well so that you can bake cookies and other treats as you're cooking things for your family. If you've got a hankering for something sweet after dinner, this is a great way to get it quickly without having to wait around with no way to satisfy the craving before the next meal is ready.

11. Saves Space

One of the greatest advantages of an air fryer is that it takes up so little space in your kitchen. Traditional ovens take up a lot of room, and for people who live in small apartments, this can be hard to handle. With an air fryer, you can put it on the counter toward the back and have all of your other kitchen appliances close by without having to worry about where they're going to go.

Guide to Cleaning & Maintenance

The dirty little secret of any air fryer is that they're not dishwasher safe. Because of the design, there's a lot of nooks and crannies that simply can't be cleaned with a dishwasher. That doesn't mean you can't wash it though! It just means you'll have to make some minor adjustments to the way you do things. The good news is that your air fryer is pretty simple and easy to take care of. Here's how to do a deep cleaning on your air fryer and maintain it year-round!

How To Clean An Air Fryer

This will involve deep cleaning your air fryer, so take care to follow these steps carefully!

1. Unplug the air fryer and remove any food particles. Then give it a good wipe down with a damp cloth or paper towel.

2. If your air fryer has a removable mesh filter, soak it in detergent and hot water to get rid of any residue from cooking

3. Use a dishwasher safe brush to clean the interior and outside of your air fryer basket. Then let it dry completely before you use it.

4. Use a cloth with mild dish soap to wash any parts of the air fryer that are not dishwasher safe.

5. Let your air fryer dry completely before using. You can't use the air fryer while it's damp!

6. If you want to keep your air fryer looking brand new, follow these simple steps every few months:

Gently scrub the exterior with a soft, nonabrasive sponge. Wipe the exterior with a damp cloth. Use a cloth with dish soap to wash any parts of your air fryer that are not dishwasher safe (like the screen and basket). Let dry completely before using.

In addition to cleaning your air fryer, you'll want to take care of it. Here's how:

How To Maintain Your Air Fryer

1. Make sure your air fryer basket is dry before you put the next batch of food in. Your food won't stick if there's no grease on the basket, and you'll have an easier time cleaning up after yourself.

2. If something spills in your air fryer, use a sponge to wipe it up. Don't use dish soap, as this can ruin the finish on your air fryer. If some food does spill in there, then it's best to empty and wipe the inside.

3. If you don't want your air fryer to get grimy, be sure to store it where it's not touching anything else when you're not using it.

4. Be sure to follow the cleaning and maintenance instructions given by your air fryer's manufacturer. These details will vary by brand!

With these simple tips, you'll be equipped to clean and maintain your air fryer any time of year.

Care Tips for Your Air Fryer

There are many people all over the world who love to cook their favorite foods with an air fryer, but there's a lot of work that goes into taking care of your new appliance. Here, I will equip you with some easy tips for caring for your air fryer. Read on.

Cleaning

Cleaning your air fryer should be done on a regular basis—preferably when you're done cooking. You should make it a habit to wash the fryer immediately after you're done cooking, before any food particles harden on the appliance. Things like grease, oil and food residue can go a long way in ruining the taste of your food if not removed on time, so always make sure to clean thoroughly every time you're done using an air fryer.

Closing The Air Fryer

Before you close up the air fryer, make sure that there's enough counter space to put the appliance in a stable position. You should also always unplug the unit before closing it, as leaving it plugged in can damage or ruin your air fryer's internal parts. Lastly, make sure not to overload your basket with too many food items, which can cause hot spots and uneven cooking times. Also, make sure the lid of the air fryer closes properly to allow even heat distribution.

Venting The Air

When you're done with cooking, be sure to vent the air fryer to release any excess heat. This can be done by opening the lid and releasing pressurized steam. Be careful, however—if you leave the lid open for too long or there are certain foods such as raw meat, it may ruin your appliance's internal parts or cause overheating or burning.

Preheating The Air Fryer

It's important to preheat your air fryer before you begin cooking. Doing so will get the oil or grease inside the appliance up to the right temperature, which will make for more consistent temperatures and faster cooking time. If you don't preheat your air fryer, the food will take a longer time to cook as it will have to struggle against cold oil or grease.

Changing The Temperature

When you change the temperature of your air fryer, make sure to do so gradually. This is to prevent sudden temperature changes that could potentially damage the appliance's internal parts and components. Another thing to remember is that doing so fast can also cause hot spots and uneven cooking times—always wait for your appliance to settle in before you start a new cooking session or decrease or increase the temperature of your appliance.

Air Fryer Frequently Asked Questions

1. How long does it take to preheat an air fryer?

Most air fryers have a preheat setting that takes about 3-5 minutes of continuous heat to get them up to the desired temperature. If you don't have continuous heat, set your temperature as high as it goes in 5-8 minutes and use the 'keep warm' setting (or wait 2 minutes) and continue cooking with the 'keep warm' setting until you're ready to cook.

2. Can I put the basket in the dishwasher?

If your basket has a non-stick coating, you definitely shouldn't put it in the dishwasher. The heat and water can cause damage to these non-stick coatings, so it's recommended to hand wash these baskets whenever possible. If you have a metal basket or stainless steel basket, then you can simply wash them by hand with warm water and soap.

3. Can I use cooking spray in an air fryer?

It can be tempting to think you can just spray the basket of an air fryer with cooking spray, but you shouldn't do this. Cooking spray will run down into the heating element, which can cause fires or damage to the heating element. It's best to cook without any oils or sprays in your air fryer.

4. Can I cook frozen foods in my air fryer?

You'll be able to cook frozen foods in your air fryer, but you may have to adjust the cooking time and temperature slightly. The reason for this is that cooked food will stay hot while frozen food cools down before it starts cooking. What you can do is set the air fryer to a lower heat setting and start it at a higher temperature, then let the freezing food sit in the basket until it warms up and starts cooking.

5. What are the essential oils in an air fryer?

The essential oil that is in an air fryer is cyclopentanone. It's the main oil that's used, but there are some models that have an extra coating of non-stick coating to make it easier to cook food without adding extra oils.

6. Can I use an air fryer for deep frying?

Air fryers have been known to be used to deep fry food, but you would have to do it very carefully. The heating element in the air fryer can overheat and start a fire if it's used too often. It's best to only use the air fryer for cooking foods that are already frozen.

7. Why is food soggy in my air fryer?

There are a few things that can make food in an air fryer soggy instead of crunchy. The most common reason for this is due to the temperature setting being too low. If the temperature is set too low, then it can cause foods to cook slowly and become soggy instead of crispy or crunchy. The next reason for soggy foods is because of water getting into the bowl. This happens when you're preheating the air fryer and setting it on the lowest setting, but don't wait long enough to let the water completely evaporate before cooking. When you do this, sometimes you might see a small pool of water in your air fryer. The final reason for soggy foods is because of food that has high moisture content such as rice, quinoa or spinach. If you have any of these foods in your air fryer, make sure they're completely dry before cooking to get the best results.

8. How often can I use my air fryer?

You can use your air fryer every day, but it will have to be cleaned before you use it again. It's best to wait at least 24 hours before using the air fryer again after you've cleaned it.

9. Can I use parchment paper in my air fryer?

You can, but you should only be using this for cooking tiny foods that won't fit in the basket. You definitely shouldn't be using parchment paper as a liner in your air fryer. This will damage the heating element and cause fires in the oven.

10. Why is my air fryer making a clicking noise?

There are a few reasons why your air fryer is making a clicking noise. First, it could be that the unit is cooling off and this is just the sound of the heating elements slowly getting cooler. It's also possible that it's the controls adjusting to your temperature settings, so it may be making this noise while you're cooking. If the unit has cooled off and continues to click, then there may be an issue with your air fryer and you should contact customer service.

Chapter 1 Breakfasts

Sausage and Egg Breakfast Burrito

Prep time: 5 minutes/ Cook time: 30 minutes / Serves 6

Ingredients :

- 6 eggs
- Salt and pepper, to taste
- Cooking oil
- 120 ml chopped red pepper
- 120 ml chopped green pepper
- 230 g chicken sausage meat (removed from casings)
- 120 ml salsa
- 6 medium (8-inch) flour tortillas
- 120 ml shredded Cheddar cheese

Preparation Instructions :

1. In a medium bowl, whisk the eggs. Add salt and pepper to taste.
2. Place a skillet on medium-high heat. Spray with cooking oil. Add the eggs. Scramble for 2 to 3 minutes, until the eggs are fluffy. Remove the eggs from the skillet and set aside.
3. If needed, spray the skillet with more oil. Add the chopped red and green bell peppers. Cook for 2 to 3 minutes, until the peppers are soft.
4. Add the sausage meat to the skillet. Break the sausage into smaller pieces using a spatula or spoon. Cook for 3 to 4 minutes, until the sausage is brown.
5. Add the salsa and scrambled eggs. Stir to combine. Remove the skillet from heat.
6. Spoon the mixture evenly onto the tortillas.
7. To form the burritos, fold the sides of each tortilla in toward the middle and then roll up from the bottom. You can secure each burrito with a toothpick. Or you can moisten the outside edge of the tortilla with a small amount of water. I prefer to use a cooking brush, but you can also dab with your fingers.
8. Spray the burritos with cooking oil and place them in the air fryer. Do not stack. Cook the burritos in batches if they do not all fit in the basket. Air fry at 204ºC for 8 minutes.
9. Open the air fryer and flip the burritos. Cook for an additional 2 minutes or until crisp.
10. If necessary, repeat steps 8 and 9 for the remaining burritos.
11. Sprinkle the Cheddar cheese over the burritos. Cool before serving.

Portobello Eggs Benedict

Prep time: 10 minutes/ Cook time: 10 to 14 minutes/ Serves 2

Ingredients :

- 1 tablespoon olive oil
- 2 cloves garlic, minced
- ¼ teaspoon dried thyme
- 2 portobello mushrooms, stems removed and gills scraped out
- 2 plum tomatoes, halved lengthwise
- Salt and freshly ground black pepper, to taste
- 2 large eggs
- 2 tablespoons grated Pecorino Romano cheese
- 1 tablespoon chopped fresh parsley, for garnish
- 1 teaspoon truffle oil (optional)

Preparation Instructions :

1. Preheat the air fryer to 204ºC.
2. In a small bowl, combine the olive oil, garlic, and thyme. Brush the mixture over the mushrooms and tomatoes until thoroughly coated. Season to taste with

salt and freshly ground black pepper.
3. Arrange the vegetables, cut side up, in the air fryer basket. Crack an egg into the center of each mushroom and sprinkle with cheese. Air fry for 10 to 14 minutes until the vegetables are tender and the whites are firm. When cool enough to handle, coarsely chop the tomatoes and place on top of the eggs. Scatter parsley on top and drizzle with truffle oil, if desired, just before serving.

Broccoli-Mushroom Frittata

Prep time: 10 minutes/ Cook time: 20 minutes/ Serves 2

Ingredients :
- 1 tablespoon olive oil
- 350 ml broccoli florets, finely chopped
- 120 ml sliced brown mushrooms
- 60 ml finely chopped onion
- ½ teaspoon salt
- ¼ teaspoon freshly ground black pepper
- 6 eggs
- 60 ml Parmesan cheese

Preparation Instructions :
1. In a nonstick cake pan, combine the olive oil, broccoli, mushrooms, onion, salt, and pepper. Stir until the vegetables are thoroughly coated with oil. Place the cake pan in the air fryer basket and set the air fryer to 204°C. Air fry for 5 minutes until the vegetables soften.
2. Meanwhile, in a medium bowl, whisk the eggs and Parmesan until thoroughly combined. Pour the egg mixture into the pan and shake gently to distribute the vegetables. Air fry for another 15 minutes until the eggs are set.
3. Remove from the air fryer and let sit for 5 minutes to cool slightly. Use a silicone spatula to gently lift the frittata onto a plate before serving.

Poached Eggs on Whole Grain Avocado Toast

Prep time: 5 minutes/ Cook time: 7 minutes/ Serves 4

Ingredients :
- Olive oil cooking spray
- 4 large eggs
- Salt
- Black pepper
- 1 avocado
- 4 pieces wholegrain bread
- Red pepper flakes (optional)

Preparation Instructions :
1. Preheat the air fryer to 160°C. Lightly coat the inside of four small oven-safe ramekins with olive oil cooking spray.
2. Crack one egg into each ramekin, and season with salt and black pepper.
3. Place the ramekins into the air fryer basket. Close and set the timer to 7 minutes.
4. While the eggs are cooking, toast the bread in a toaster.
5. Slice the avocado in half lengthwise, remove the pit, and scoop the flesh into a small bowl. Season with salt, black pepper, and red pepper flakes, if desired. Using a fork, smash the avocado lightly.
6. Spread a quarter of the smashed avocado evenly over each slice of toast.
7. Remove the eggs from the air fryer, and gently spoon one onto each slice of avocado toast before serving.

Cheddar Eggs

Prep time: 5 minutes/ Cook time: 15 minutes/ Serves 2

Ingredients :
- 4 large eggs

- 2 tablespoons unsalted butter, melted
- 120 ml shredded sharp Cheddar cheese

Preparation Instructions :

1. Crack eggs into a round baking dish and whisk. Place dish into the air fryer basket.
2. Adjust the temperature to 204°C and set the timer for 10 minutes.
3. After 5 minutes, stir the eggs and add the butter and cheese. Let cook 3 more minutes and stir again.
4. Allow eggs to finish cooking an additional 2 minutes or remove if they are to your desired liking.
5. Use a fork to fluff. Serve warm.

Golden Avocado Tempura

Prep time: 5 minutes/ Cook time: 10 minutes/ Serves 4

Ingredients :

- 120 ml bread crumbs
- ½ teaspoons salt
- 1 Haas avocado, pitted, peeled and sliced
- Liquid from 1 can white beans

Preparation Instructions :

1. Preheat the air fryer to 176°C.
2. Mix the bread crumbs and salt in a shallow bowl until well-incorporated.
3. Dip the avocado slices in the bean liquid, then into the bread crumbs.
4. Put the avocados in the air fryer, taking care not to overlap any slices, and air fry for 10 minutes, giving the basket a good shake at the halfway point.
5. Serve immediately.

Parmesan Ranch Risotto

Prep time: 10 minutes/ Cook time: 30 minutes/ Serves 2

Ingredients :

- 1 tablespoon olive oil
- 1 clove garlic, minced
- 1 tablespoon unsalted butter
- 1 onion, diced
- 180 ml Arborio rice
- 475 ml chicken stock, boiling
- 120 ml Parmesan cheese, grated

Preparation Instructions :

1. Preheat the air fryer to 200°C.
2. Grease a round baking tin with olive oil and stir in the garlic, butter, and onion.
3. Transfer the tin to the air fryer and bake for 4 minutes. Add the rice and bake for 4 more minutes.
4. Turn the air fryer to 160°C and pour in the chicken stock. Cover and bake for 22 minutes.
5. Scatter with cheese and serve.

Spinach Omelet

Prep time: 5 minutes/ Cook time: 12 minutes/ Serves 2

Ingredients :

- 4 large eggs
- 350 ml chopped fresh spinach leaves
- 2 tablespoons peeled and chopped brown onion
- 2 tablespoons salted butter, melted
- 120 ml shredded mild Cheddar cheese
- ¼ teaspoon salt

Preparation Instructions :

1. In an ungreased round nonstick baking dish, whisk eggs. Stir in spinach, onion, butter, Cheddar, and salt.
2. Place dish into air fryer basket. Adjust the temperature to 160°C and bake for 12 minutes. Omelet will be done when browned on the top and firm in the middle.
3. Slice in half and serve warm on two medium plates.

Buffalo Egg Cups

Prep time: 10 minutes/ Cook time: 15 minutes/ Serves 2

Ingredients :
- 4 large eggs
- 60 g full-fat cream cheese
- 2 tablespoons buffalo sauce
- 120 ml shredded sharp Cheddar cheese

Preparation Instructions :
1. Crack eggs into two ramekins.
2. In a small microwave-safe bowl, mix cream cheese, buffalo sauce, and Cheddar. Microwave for 20 seconds and then stir. Place a spoonful into each ramekin on top of the eggs.
3. Place ramekins into the air fryer basket.
4. Adjust the temperature to 160°C and bake for 15 minutes.
5. Serve warm.

Tomato and Cheddar Rolls

Prep time: 30 minutes/ Cook time: 25 minutes/ Makes 12 rolls

Ingredients :
- 4 plum tomatoes
- ½ clove garlic, minced
- 1 tablespoon olive oil
- ¼ teaspoon dried thyme
- Salt and freshly ground black pepper, to taste
- 1 L plain flour
- 1 teaspoon active dry yeast
- 2 teaspoons sugar
- 2 teaspoons salt
- 1 tablespoon olive oil
- 235 ml grated Cheddar cheese, plus more for sprinkling at the end
- 350 ml water

Preparation Instructions :
1. Cut the tomatoes in half, remove the seeds with your fingers and transfer to a bowl. Add the garlic, olive oil, dried thyme, salt and freshly ground black pepper and toss well.
2. Preheat the air fryer to 200°C.
3. Place the tomatoes, cut side up in the air fryer basket and air fry for 10 minutes. The tomatoes should just start to brown. Shake the basket to redistribute the tomatoes, and air fry for another 5 to 10 minutes at 166°C until the tomatoes are no longer juicy. Let the tomatoes cool and then rough chop them.
4. Combine the flour, yeast, sugar and salt in the bowl of a stand mixer. Add the olive oil, chopped roasted tomatoes and Cheddar cheese to the flour mixture and start to mix using the dough hook attachment. As you're mixing, add 300 ml of the water, mixing until the dough comes together. Continue to knead the dough with the dough hook for another 10 minutes, adding enough water to the dough to get it to the right consistency.
5. Transfer the dough to an oiled bowl, cover with a clean kitchen towel and let it rest and rise until it has doubled in volume, about 1 to 2 hours. Then, divide the dough into 12 equal portions. Roll each portion of dough into a ball. Lightly coat each dough ball with oil and let the dough balls rest and rise a second time, covered lightly with plastic wrap for 45 minutes. (Alternately, you can place the rolls in the refrigerator overnight and take them out 2 hours before you bake them.)
6. Preheat the air fryer to 182°C.
7. Spray the dough balls and the air fryer basket with a little olive oil. Place three rolls at a time in the basket and bake for 10 minutes. Add a little grated Cheddar cheese on top of the rolls for the last 2 minutes of air frying for an attractive finish.

Sausage and Cheese Balls

Prep time: 10 minutes/ Cook time: 12 minutes/ Makes 16 balls

Ingredients :

- 450 g pork sausage meat, removed from casings
- 120 ml shredded Cheddar cheese
- 30 g full-fat cream cheese, softened
- 1 large egg

Preparation Instructions :

1. Mix all ingredients in a large bowl. Form into sixteen (1-inch) balls. Place the balls into the air fryer basket.
2. Adjust the temperature to 204°C and air fry for 12 minutes.
3. Shake the basket two or three times during cooking. Sausage balls will be browned on the outside and have an internal temperature of at least 64°C when completely cooked.
4. Serve warm.

Bourbon Vanilla French Toast

Prep time: 15 minutes/ Cook time: 6 minutes/ Serves 4

Ingredients :

- 2 large eggs
- 2 tablespoons water
- 160 ml whole or semi-skimmed milk
- 1 tablespoon butter, melted
- 2 tablespoons bourbon
- 1 teaspoon vanilla extract
- 8 (1-inch-thick) French bread slices
- Cooking spray

Preparation Instructions :

1. Preheat the air fryer to 160°C. Line the air fryer basket with parchment paper and spray it with cooking spray.
2. Beat the eggs with the water in a shallow bowl until combined. Add the milk, melted butter, bourbon, and vanilla and stir to mix well.
3. Dredge 4 slices of bread in the batter, turning to coat both sides evenly. Transfer the bread slices onto the parchment paper.
4. Bake for 6 minutes until nicely browned. Flip the slices halfway through the cooking time.
5. Remove from the basket to a plate and repeat with the remaining 4 slices of bread.
6. Serve warm.

Cajun Breakfast Sausage

Prep time: 10 minutes/ Cook time: 15 to 20 minutes/ Serves 8

Ingredients :

- 680 g 85% lean turkey mince
- 3 cloves garlic, finely chopped
- ¼ onion, grated
- 1 teaspoon Tabasco sauce
- 1 teaspoon Cajun seasoning
- 1 teaspoon dried thyme
- ½ teaspoon paprika
- ½ teaspoon cayenne

Preparation Instructions :

1. Preheat the air fryer to 188°C.
2. In a large bowl, combine the turkey, garlic, onion, Tabasco, Cajun seasoning, thyme, paprika, and cayenne. Mix with clean hands until thoroughly combined. Shape into 16 patties, about ½ inch thick. (Wet your hands slightly if you find the sausage too sticky to handle.)
3. Working in batches if necessary, arrange the patties in a single layer in the air fryer basket. Pausing halfway through the cooking time to flip the patties, air fry for 15

to 20 minutes until a thermometer inserted into the thickest portion registers 74ºC.

Gluten-Free Granola Cereal

Prep time: 7 minutes/ Cook time: 30 minutes/ Makes 820 ml

Ingredients :

- Oil, for spraying
- 350 ml gluten-free rolled oats
- 120 ml chopped walnuts
- 120 ml chopped almonds
- 120 ml pumpkin seeds
- 60 ml maple syrup or honey
- 1 tablespoon toasted sesame oil or vegetable oil
- 1 teaspoon ground cinnamon
- ½ teaspoon salt
- 120 ml dried cranberries

Preparation Instructions :

1. Preheat the air fryer to 120ºC. Line the air fryer basket with parchment and spray lightly with oil. (Do not skip the step of lining the basket; the parchment will keep the granola from falling through the holes.)
2. In a large bowl, mix together the oats, walnuts, almonds, pumpkin seeds, maple syrup, sesame oil, cinnamon, and salt.
3. Spread the mixture in an even layer in the prepared basket.
4. Cook for 30 minutes, stirring every 10 minutes.
5. Transfer the granola to a bowl, add the dried cranberries, and toss to combine.
6. Let cool to room temperature before storing in an airtight container.

Western Frittata

Prep time: 10 minutes/ Cook time: 19 minutes/ Serves 1 to 2

Ingredients :

- ½ red or green pepper, cut into ½-inch chunks
- 1 teaspoon olive oil
- 3 eggs, beaten
- 60 ml grated Cheddar cheese
- 60 ml diced cooked ham
- Salt and freshly ground black pepper, to taste
- 1 teaspoon butter
- 1 teaspoon chopped fresh parsley

Preparation Instructions :

1. Preheat the air fryer to 204ºC.
2. Toss the peppers with the olive oil and air fry for 6 minutes, shaking the basket once or twice during the cooking process to redistribute the ingredients.
3. While the vegetables are cooking, beat the eggs well in a bowl, stir in the Cheddar cheese and ham, and season with salt and freshly ground black pepper. Add the air-fried peppers to this bowl when they have finished cooking.
4. Place a cake pan into the air fryer basket with the butter using an aluminum sling to lower the pan into the basket. Air fry for 1 minute at 192ºC to melt the butter. Remove the cake pan and rotate the pan to distribute the butter and grease the pan. Pour the egg mixture into the cake pan and return the pan to the air fryer, using the aluminum sling.
5. Air fry at 192ºC for 12 minutes, or until the frittata has puffed up and is lightly browned. Let the frittata sit in the air fryer for 5 minutes to cool to an edible temperature and set up. Remove the cake pan from the air fryer, sprinkle with parsley and serve immediately.

Jalapeño and Bacon Breakfast Pizza

Prep time: 5 minutes/ Cook time: 10 minutes/ Serves 2

Ingredients :

- 235 ml shredded Mozzarella cheese

- 30 g cream cheese, broken into small pieces
- 4 slices cooked bacon, chopped
- 60 ml chopped pickled jalapeños
- 1 large egg, whisked
- ¼ teaspoon salt

Preparation Instructions :

1. Place Mozzarella in a single layer on the bottom of an ungreased round nonstick baking dish. Scatter cream cheese pieces, bacon, and jalapeños over Mozzarella, then pour egg evenly around baking dish.
2. Sprinkle with salt and place into air fryer basket. Adjust the temperature to 166°C and bake for 10 minutes. When cheese is brown and egg is set, pizza will be done.
3. Let cool on a large plate 5 minutes before serving.

Honey-Apricot Granola with Greek Yoghurt

Prep time: 10 minutes/ Cook time: 30 minutes / Serves 6

Ingredients :

- 235 ml rolled oats
- 60 ml dried apricots, diced
- 60 ml almond slivers
- 60 ml walnuts, chopped
- 60 ml pumpkin seeds
- 60 to 80 ml honey, plus more for drizzling
- 1 tablespoon olive oil
- 1 teaspoon ground cinnamon
- ¼ teaspoon ground nutmeg
- ¼ teaspoon salt
- 2 tablespoons sugar-free dark chocolate chips (optional)
- 700 ml fat-free plain Greek yoghurt

Preparation Instructions :

1. Preheat the air fryer to 128°C. Line the air fryer basket with parchment paper.
2. In a large bowl, combine the oats, apricots, almonds, walnuts, pumpkin seeds, honey, olive oil, cinnamon, nutmeg, and salt, mixing so that the honey, oil, and spices are well distributed.
3. Pour the mixture onto the parchment paper and spread it into an even layer.
4. Bake for 10 minutes, then shake or stir and spread back out into an even layer. Continue baking for 10 minutes more, then repeat the process of shaking or stirring the mixture. Bake for an additional 10 minutes before removing from the air fryer.
5. Allow the granola to cool completely before stirring in the chocolate chips (if using) and pouring into an airtight container for storage.
6. For each serving, top 120 ml Greek yoghurt with 80 ml granola and a drizzle of honey, if needed.

Banana-Nut Muffins

Prep time: 5 minutes/ Cook time: 15 minutes/ Makes 10 muffins

Ingredients :

- Oil, for spraying
- 2 very ripe bananas
- 120 ml packed light brown sugar
- 80 ml rapeseed oil or vegetable oil
- 1 large egg
- 1 teaspoon vanilla extract
- 180 ml plain flour
- 1 teaspoon baking powder
- 1 teaspoon ground cinnamon
- 120 ml chopped walnuts

Preparation Instructions :

1. Preheat the air fryer to 160°C. Spray 10 silicone muffin cups lightly with oil.
2. In a medium bowl, mash the bananas. Add the brown sugar, rapeseed oil, egg,

and vanilla and stir to combine.
3. Fold in the flour, baking powder, and cinnamon until just combined.
4. Add the walnuts and fold a few times to distribute throughout the batter.
5. Divide the batter equally among the prepared muffin cups and place them in the basket. You may need to work in batches, depending on the size of your air fryer.
6. Cook for 15 minutes, or until golden brown and a toothpick inserted into the center of a muffin comes out clean. The air fryer tends to brown muffins more than the oven, so don't be alarmed if they are darker than you're used to. They will still taste great.
7. Let cool on a wire rack before serving.

French Toast Sticks

Prep time: 10 minutes/ Cook time: 9 minutes/ Serves 4

Ingredients :
- Oil, for spraying
- 6 large eggs
- 315 ml milk
- 2 teaspoons vanilla extract
- 1 teaspoon ground cinnamon
- 8 slices bread, cut into thirds
- Syrup of choice, for serving

Preparation Instructions :
1. Preheat the air fryer to 188°C. Line the air fryer basket with parchment and spray lightly with oil.
2. In a shallow bowl, whisk the eggs, milk, vanilla, and cinnamon.
3. Dunk one piece of bread in the egg mixture, making sure to coat both sides. Work quickly so the bread doesn't get soggy. Immediately transfer the bread to the prepared basket.
4. Repeat with the remaining bread, making sure the pieces don't touch each other. You may need to work in batches, depending on the size of your air fryer.
5. Air fry for 5 minutes, flip, and cook for another 3 to 4 minutes, until browned and crispy.
6. Serve immediately with your favorite syrup.

Oat Bran Muffins

Prep time: 10 minutes/ Cook time: 10 to 12 minutes per batch/ Makes 8 muffins

Ingredients :
- 160 ml oat bran
- 120 ml flour
- 60 ml brown sugar
- 1 egg
- 1 teaspoon baking powder
- ½ teaspoon baking soda
- ⅛ teaspoon salt
- 120 ml buttermilk
- 2 tablespoons rapeseed oil
- 120 ml chopped dates, raisins, or dried cranberries
- 24 paper muffin cups
- Cooking spray

Preparation Instructions :
1. Preheat the air fryer to 166°C.
2. In a large bowl, combine the oat bran, flour, brown sugar, baking powder, baking soda, and salt.
3. In a small bowl, beat together the buttermilk, egg, and oil.
4. Pour buttermilk mixture into bowl with dry ingredients and stir just until moistened. Do not beat.
5. Gently stir in dried fruit.
6. Use triple baking cups to help muffins hold shape during baking. Spray them with cooking spray, place 4 sets of cups in air fryer basket at a time, and fill each one ¾ full of batter.
7. Cook for 10 to 12 minutes, until top springs back when lightly touched and toothpick inserted in center comes out clean.
8. Repeat for remaining muffins.

Chapter 2 Fast and Easy Everyday Favourites

Spinach and Carrot Balls

Prep time: 10 minutes/ Cook time: 10 minutes/ Serves 4

Ingredients :
- 2 slices toasted bread
- 1 carrot, peeled and grated
- 1 package fresh spinach, blanched and chopped
- ½ onion, chopped
- 1 egg, beaten
- ½ teaspoon garlic powder
- 1 teaspoon minced garlic
- 1 teaspoon salt
- ½ teaspoon black pepper
- 1 tablespoon Engevita yeast flakes
- 1 tablespoon flour

Preparation Instructions :
1. Preheat the air fryer to 200ºC.
2. In a food processor, pulse the toasted bread to form breadcrumbs. Transfer into a shallow dish or bowl.
3. In a bowl, mix together all the other ingredients. Use your hands to shape the mixture into small-sized balls. Roll the balls in the breadcrumbs, ensuring to cover them well. Put in the air fryer basket and air fry for 10 minutes.
4. Serve immediately.

Beery and Crunchy Onion Rings

Prep time: 10 minutes/ Cook time: 16 minutes/ Serves 2 to 4

Ingredients :
- 160 ml plain flour
- 1 teaspoon paprika
- ½ teaspoon bicarbonate of soda
- 1 teaspoon salt
- ½ teaspoon freshly ground black pepper
- 1 egg, beaten
- 180 ml beer
- 350 ml breadcrumbs
- 1 tablespoons olive oil
- 1 large Vidalia or sweet onion, peeled and sliced into ½-inch rings
- Cooking spray

Preparation Instructions :
1. Preheat the air fryer to 182ºC.
2. Spritz the air fryer basket with cooking spray. Combine the flour, paprika, bicarbonate of soda, salt, and ground black pepper in a bowl. Stir to mix well.
3. Combine the egg and beer in a separate bowl. Stir to mix well. Make a well in the centre of the flour mixture, then pour the egg mixture in the well. Stir to mix everything well. Pour the breadcrumbs and olive oil in a shallow plate. Stir to mix well. Dredge the onion rings gently into the flour and egg mixture, then shake the excess off and put into the plate of breadcrumbs.
4. Flip to coat both sides well. Arrange the onion rings in the preheated air fryer. Air fry in batches for 16 minutes or until golden brown and crunchy. Flip the rings and put the bottom rings to the top halfway through.
5. Serve immediately.

Simple Pea Delight

Prep time: 5 minutes/ Cook time: 15 minutes/

Serves 2 to 4

Ingredients :
- 235 ml flour
- 1 teaspoon baking powder
- 3 eggs
- 235 ml coconut milk
- 235 ml soft white cheese
- 3 tablespoons pea protein
- 120 ml chicken or turkey strips
- Pinch of sea salt
- 235 ml Mozzarella cheese

Preparation Instructions :
1. Preheat the air fryer to 200°C.
2. In a large bowl, mix all ingredients together using a large wooden spoon. Spoon equal amounts of the mixture into muffin cups and bake for 15 minutes.
3. Serve immediately.

Air Fried Courgette Sticks

Prep time: 5 minutes/ Cook time: 20 minutes/ Serves 4

Ingredients :
- 1 medium courgette, cut into 48 sticks
- 60 ml seasoned breadcrumbs
- 1 tablespoon melted margarine
- Cooking spray

Preparation Instructions :
1. Preheat the air fryer to 182°C. Spritz the air fryer basket with cooking spray and set aside.
2. In 2 different shallow bowls, add the seasoned breadcrumbs and the margarine. One by one, dredge the courgette sticks into the margarine, then roll in the breadcrumbs to coat evenly.
3. Arrange the crusted sticks on a plate. Place the courgette sticks in the prepared air fryer basket. Work in two batches to avoid overcrowding. Air fry for 10 minutes, or until golden brown and crispy. Shake the basket halfway through to cook evenly.
4. When the cooking time is over, transfer the fries to a wire rack. Rest for 5 minutes and serve warm.

Bacon Pinwheels

Prep time: 10 minutes/ Cook time: 10 minutes/ Makes 8 pinwheels

Ingredients :
- 1 sheet puff pastry
- 2 tablespoons maple syrup
- 60 ml brown sugar
- 8 slices bacon
- Ground black pepper, to taste
- Cooking spray

Preparation Instructions :
1. Preheat the air fryer to 182°C. Spritz the air fryer basket with cooking spray.
2. Roll the puff pastry into a 10-inch square with a rolling pin on a clean work surface, then cut the pastry into 8 strips. Brush the strips with maple syrup and sprinkle with sugar, leaving a 1-inch far end uncovered.
3. Arrange each slice of bacon on each strip, leaving a ⅛-inch length of bacon hang over the end close to you. Sprinkle with black pepper. From the end close to you, roll the strips into pinwheels, then dab the uncovered end with water and seal the rolls.
4. Arrange the pinwheels in the preheated air fryer and spritz with cooking spray. Air fry for 10 minutes or until golden brown. Flip the pinwheels halfway through.
5. Serve immediately.

Air Fried Shishito Peppers

Prep time: 5 minutes/ Cook time: 5 minutes/

Serves 4

Ingredients :

- 230 g shishito or Padron peppers (about 24)
- 1 tablespoon olive oil
- Coarse sea salt, to taste
- Lemon wedges, for serving
- Cooking spray

Preparation Instructions :

1. Preheat the air fryer to 204°C. Spritz the air fryer basket with cooking spray.
2. Toss the peppers with olive oil in a large bowl to coat well. Arrange the peppers in the preheated air fryer. Air fryer for 5 minutes or until blistered and lightly charred.
3. Shake the basket and sprinkle the peppers with salt halfway through the cooking time.
4. Transfer the peppers onto a plate and squeeze the lemon wedges on top before serving.

Beetroot Salad with Lemon Vinaigrette

Prep time: 10 minutes/ Cook time: 12 to 15 minutes/ Serves 4

Ingredients :

- 6 medium red and golden beetroots, peeled and sliced
- 1 teaspoon olive oil
- ¼ teaspoon rock salt
- 120 ml crumbled feta cheese
- 2 L mixed greens
- Cooking spray

Vinaigrette:

- 2 teaspoons olive oil
- 2 tablespoons chopped fresh chives
- Juice of 1 lemon

Preparation Instructions :

1. Preheat the air fryer to 182°C.
2. In a large bowl, toss the beetroots, olive oil, and rock salt. Spray the air fryer basket with cooking spray, then place the beetroots in the basket and air fry for 12 to 15 minutes or until tender.
3. While the beetroots cook, make the vinaigrette in a large bowl by whisking together the olive oil, lemon juice, and chives. Remove the beetroots from the air fryer, toss in the vinaigrette, and allow to cool for 5 minutes.
4. Add the feta and serve on top of the mixed greens.

Herb-Roasted Veggies

Prep time: 10 minutes/ Cook time: 14 to 18 minutes/ Serves 4

Ingredients :

- 1 red pepper, sliced
- 1 (230 g) package sliced mushrooms
- 235 ml green beans, cut into 2-inch pieces
- 80 ml diced red onion
- 3 garlic cloves, sliced
- 1 teaspoon olive oil
- ½ teaspoon dried basil
- ½ teaspoon dried tarragon

Preparation Instructions :

1. Preheat the air fryer to 200°C.
2. Cut the slices of bread into medium-size chunks.
3. Brush the air fryer basket with the oil. Place the chunks inside and air fry for at least 8 minutes.
4. Serve with hot soup.

Simple and Easy Croutons

Prep time: 5 minutes/ Cook time: 8 minutes/ Serves 4

Ingredients :

- 2 slices bread

- 1 tablespoon olive oil
- Hot soup, for serving

Preparation Instructions :
1. Preheat the air fryer to 200°C.
2. Cut the slices of bread into medium-size chunks. Brush the air fryer basket with the oil.
3. Place the chunks inside and air fry for at least 8 minutes.
4. Serve with hot soup.

Corn Fritters

Prep time: 15 minutes/ Cook time: 8 minutes / Serves 6

Ingredients :
- 235 ml self-raising flour
- 1 tablespoon sugar
- 1 teaspoon salt
- 1 large egg, lightly beaten
- 60 ml buttermilk
- 180 ml corn kernels
- 60 ml minced onion
- Cooking spray

Preparation Instructions :
1. Preheat the air fryer to 176°C. Line the air fryer basket with parchment paper.
2. In a medium bowl, whisk the flour, sugar, and salt until blended. Stir in the egg and buttermilk. Add the corn and minced onion. Mix well. Shape the corn fritter batter into 12 balls.
3. Place the fritters on the parchment and spritz with oil. Bake for 4 minutes.
4. Flip the fritters, spritz them with oil, and bake for 4 minutes more until firm and lightly browned.
5. Serve immediately.

Easy Devils on Horseback

Prep time: 5 minutes/ Cook time: 7 minutes/ Serves 12

Ingredients :
- 24 small pitted prunes (128 g)
- 60 ml crumbled blue cheese, divided
- 8 slices centre-cut bacon, cut crosswise into thirds

Preparation Instructions :
1. Preheat the air fryer to 204°C.
2. Halve the prunes lengthwise, but don't cut them all the way through. Place ½ teaspoon of cheese in the centre of each prune. Wrap a piece of bacon around each prune and secure the bacon with a toothpick.
3. Working in batches, arrange a single layer of the prunes in the air fryer basket. Air fry for about 7 minutes, flipping halfway, until the bacon is cooked through and crisp.
4. Let cool slightly and serve warm.

Peppery Brown Rice Fritters

Prep time: 10 minutes/ Cook time: 8 to 10 minutes/ Serves 4

Ingredients :
- 1 (284 g) bag frozen cooked brown rice, thawed
- 1 egg
- 3 tablespoons brown rice flour
- 80 ml finely grated carrots
- 80 ml minced red pepper
- 2 tablespoons minced fresh basil
- 3 tablespoons grated Parmesan cheese
- 2 teaspoons olive oil

Preparation Instructions :
1. Preheat the air fryer to 192°C.

2. In a small bowl, combine the thawed rice, egg, and flour and mix to blend. Stir in the carrots, pepper, basil, and Parmesan cheese.
3. Form the mixture into 8 fritters and drizzle with the olive oil.
4. Put the fritters carefully into the air fryer basket. Air fry for 8 to 10 minutes, or until the fritters are golden brown and cooked through.
5. Serve immediately.

Rosemary and Orange Roasted Chickpeas

Prep time: 5 minutes/ Cook time: 10 to 12 minutes/ Makes 1 L

Ingredients :

- 1 L cooked chickpeas
- 2 tablespoons vegetable oil
- 1 teaspoon rock salt
- 1 teaspoon cumin
- 1 teaspoon paprika
- Zest of 1 orange
- 1 tablespoon chopped fresh rosemary

Preparation Instructions :

1. Preheat the air fryer to 204°C. Make sure the chickpeas are completely dry prior to roasting.
2. In a medium bowl, toss the chickpeas with oil, salt, cumin, and paprika.
3. Working in batches, spread the chickpeas in a single layer in the air fryer basket. Air fry for 10 to 12 minutes until crisp, shaking once halfway through.
4. Return the warm chickpeas to the bowl and toss with the orange zest and rosemary.
5. Allow to cool completely. Serve.

Easy Roasted Asparagus

Prep time: 5 minutes/ Cook time: 6 minutes/ Serves 4

Ingredients :

- 450 g asparagus, trimmed and halved crosswise
- 1 teaspoon extra-virgin olive oil
- Salt and pepper, to taste
- Lemon wedges, for serving

Preparation Instructions :

1. Preheat the air fryer to 204°C.
2. Toss the asparagus with the oil, ⅛ teaspoon salt, and ⅛ teaspoon pepper in bowl. Transfer to air fryer basket.
3. Place the basket in air fryer and roast for 6 to 8 minutes, or until tender and bright green, tossing halfway through cooking.
4. Season with salt and pepper and serve with lemon wedges.

Chapter 3 Poultry

Buttermilk-Fried Drumsticks

Prep time: 10 minutes/ Cook time: 25 minutes/ Serves 2

Ingredients :
- 1 egg
- 120 g buttermilk
- 90 g self-rising flour
- 90 g seasoned panko bread crumbs
- 1 teaspoon salt
- ¼ teaspoon ground black pepper (to mix into coating)
- 4 chicken drumsticks, skin on
- Oil for misting or cooking spray

Preparation Instructions :
1. Beat together egg and buttermilk in shallow dish.
2. In a second shallow dish, combine the flour, panko crumbs, salt, and pepper.
3. Sprinkle chicken legs with additional salt and pepper to taste.
4. Dip legs in buttermilk mixture, then roll in panko mixture, pressing in crumbs to make coating stick. Mist with oil or cooking spray.
5. Spray the air fryer basket with cooking spray.
6. Cook drumsticks at 180°C for 10 minutes. Turn pieces over and cook an additional 10 minutes.
7. Turn pieces to check for browning. If you have any white spots that haven't begun to brown, spritz them with oil or cooking spray. Continue cooking for 5 more minutes or until crust is golden brown and juices run clear. Larger, meatier drumsticks will take longer to cook than small ones.

Sriracha-Honey Chicken Nuggets

Prep time: 15 minutes/ Cook time: 19 minutes / Serves 6

Ingredients :
- Oil, for spraying
- 1 large egg
- 180 ml milk
- 125 g all-purpose flour
- 2 tablespoons icing sugar
- ½ teaspoon paprika
- ½ teaspoon salt
- ½ teaspoon freshly ground black pepper
- 2 boneless, skinless chicken breasts, cut into bite-size pieces
- 140 g barbecue sauce
- 2 tablespoons honey
- 1 tablespoon Sriracha

Preparation Instructions :
1. Line the air fryer basket with parchment and spray lightly with oil.
2. In a small bowl, whisk together the egg and milk.
3. In a medium bowl, combine the flour, icing sugar, paprika, salt, and black pepper and stir.
4. Coat the chicken in the egg mixture, then dredge in the flour mixture until evenly coated.
5. Place the chicken in the prepared basket and spray liberally with oil.
6. Air fry at 200°C for 8 minutes, flip, spray with more oil, and cook for another 6 to 8 minutes, or until the internal temperature

reaches 76ºC and the juices run clear.
7. In a large bowl, mix together the barbecue sauce, honey, and Sriracha.
8. Transfer the chicken to the bowl and toss until well coated with the barbecue sauce mixture.
9. Line the air fryer basket with fresh parchment, return the chicken to the basket, and cook for another 2 to 3 minutes, until browned and crispy.

Buffalo Chicken Cheese Sticks

Prep time: 5 minutes/ Cook time: 8 minutes/ Serves 2

Ingredients :
- 140 g shredded cooked chicken
- 60 ml buffalo sauce
- 220 g shredded Mozzarella cheese
- 1 large egg
- 55 g crumbled feta

Preparation Instructions :
1. In a large bowl, mix all ingredients except the feta. Cut a piece of parchment to fit your air fryer basket and press the mixture into a ½-inch-thick circle.
2. Sprinkle the mixture with feta and place into the air fryer basket.
3. Adjust the temperature to 200ºC and air fry for 8 minutes.
4. After 5 minutes, flip over the cheese mixture.
5. Allow to cool 5 minutes before cutting into sticks. Serve warm.

Turkey Meatloaf

Prep time: 10 minutes/ Cook time: 50 minutes/ Serves 4

Ingredients :
- 230 g sliced mushrooms
- 1 small onion, coarsely chopped
- 2 cloves garlic
- 680 g 85% lean turkey mince
- 2 eggs, lightly beaten
- 1 tablespoon tomato paste
- 25 g almond meal
- 2 tablespoons almond milk
- 1 tablespoon dried oregano
- 1 teaspoon salt
- ½ teaspoon freshly ground black pepper
- 1 Roma tomato, thinly sliced

Preparation Instructions :
1. Preheat the air fryer to 180ºC. . Lightly coat a round pan with olive oil and set aside.
2. In a food processor fitted with a metal blade, combine the mushrooms, onion, and garlic. Pulse until finely chopped. Transfer the vegetables to a large mixing bowl.
3. Add the turkey, eggs, tomato paste, almond meal, milk, oregano, salt, and black pepper. Mix gently until thoroughly combined. Transfer the mixture to the prepared pan and shape into a loaf. Arrange the tomato slices on top.
4. Air fry for 50 minutes or until the meatloaf is nicely browned and a thermometer inserted into the thickest part registers 76ºC. Remove from the air fryer and let rest for about 10 minutes before slicing.

Italian Crispy Chicken

Prep time: 10 minutes/ Cook time: 20 minutes/ Serves 4

Ingredients :
- 2 (115 g) boneless, skinless chicken breasts
- 2 egg whites, beaten
- 120 g Italian bread crumbs
- 45 g grated Parmesan cheese

- 2 teaspoons Italian seasoning
- Salt and freshly ground black pepper, to taste
- Cooking oil spray
- 180 g marinara sauce
- 110 g shredded Mozzarella cheese

Preparation Instructions :

1. With your knife blade parallel to the cutting board, cut the chicken breasts in half horizontally to create 4 thin cutlets. On a solid surface, pound the cutlets to flatten them. You can use your hands, a rolling pin, a kitchen mallet, or a meat hammer.
2. Pour the egg whites into a bowl large enough to dip the chicken.
3. In another bowl large enough to dip a chicken cutlet in, stir together the bread crumbs, Parmesan cheese, and Italian seasoning, and season with salt and pepper.
4. Dip each cutlet into the egg whites and into the breadcrumb mixture to coat.
5. Insert the crisper plate into the basket and the basket into the unit. Preheat the unit by selecting AIR FRY, setting the temperature to 190ºC, and setting the time to 3 minutes. Select START/STOP to begin.
6. Once the unit is preheated, spray the crisper plate with cooking oil. Working in batches, place 2 chicken cutlets into the basket. Spray the top of the chicken with cooking oil.
7. Select AIR FRY, set the temperature to 190ºC, and set the time to 7 minutes. Select START/STOP to begin.
8. When the cooking is complete, repeat steps 6 and 7 with the remaining cutlets.
9. Top the chicken cutlets with the marinara sauce and shredded Mozzarella cheese. If the chicken will fit into the basket without stacking, you can prepare all 4 at once. Otherwise, do this 2 cutlets at a time.
10. Select AIR FRY, set the temperature to 190ºC, and set the time to 3 minutes. Select START/STOP to begin.
11. The cooking is complete when the cheese is melted and the chicken reaches an internal temperature of 76ºC. Cool for 5 minutes before serving.

Crisp Paprika Chicken Drumsticks

Prep time: 5 minutes/ Cook time: 22 minutes/ Serves 2

Ingredients :

- 2 teaspoons paprika
- 1 teaspoon packed brown sugar
- 1 teaspoon garlic powder
- ½ teaspoon dry mustard
- ½ teaspoon salt
- Pinch pepper
- 4 (140 g) chicken drumsticks, trimmed
- 1 teaspoon vegetable oil
- 1 scallion, green part only, sliced thin on bias

Preparation Instructions :

1. Preheat the air fryer to 200ºC.
2. Combine paprika, sugar, garlic powder, mustard, salt, and pepper in a bowl. Pat drumsticks dry with paper towels. Using metal skewer, poke 10 to 15 holes in skin of each drumstick. Rub with oil and sprinkle evenly with spice mixture.
3. Arrange drumsticks in air fryer basket, spaced evenly apart, alternating ends. Air fry until chicken is crisp and registers 90ºC, 22 to 25 minutes, flipping chicken halfway through cooking.
4. Transfer chicken to serving platter, tent loosely with aluminum foil, and let rest for 5 minutes. Sprinkle with scallion and serve.

Lettuce-Wrapped Turkey and Mushroom Meatballs

Prep time: 10 minutes/ Cook time: 15 minutes / Serves 6

Ingredients :

Sauce:
- 2 tablespoons tamari
- 2 tablespoons tomato sauce
- 1 tablespoon lime juice
- ¼ teaspoon peeled and grated fresh ginger
- 1 clove garlic, smashed to a paste
- 120 ml chicken broth
- 70 g sugar
- 2 tablespoons toasted sesame oil
- Cooking spray

Meatballs:
- 900 g turkey mince
- 75 g finely chopped button mushrooms
- 2 large eggs, beaten
- 1½ teaspoons tamari
- 15 g finely chopped green onions, plus more for garnish
- 2 teaspoons peeled and grated fresh ginger
- 1 clove garlic, smashed
- 2 teaspoons toasted sesame oil
- 2 tablespoons sugar

For Serving:
- Lettuce leaves, for serving
- Sliced red chilies, for garnish (optional)
- Toasted sesame seeds, for garnish (optional)

Preparation Instructions :

1. Preheat the air fryer to 180ºC. Spritz a baking pan with cooking spray.
2. Combine the ingredients for the sauce in a small bowl. Stir to mix well. Set aside.
3. Combine the ingredients for the meatballs in a large bowl. Stir to mix well, then shape the mixture in twelve 1½-inch meatballs.
4. Arrange the meatballs in a single layer on the baking pan, then baste with the sauce. You may need to work in batches to avoid overcrowding.
5. Arrange the pan in the air fryer. Air fry for 15 minutes or until the meatballs are golden brown. Flip the balls halfway through the cooking time.
6. Unfold the lettuce leaves on a large serving plate, then transfer the cooked meatballs on the leaves. Spread the red chilies and sesame seeds over the balls, then serve.

Jalapeño Popper Hasselback Chicken

Prep time: 10 minutes/ Cook time: 19 minutes/ Serves 2

Ingredients :

- Oil, for spraying
- 2 (230 g) boneless, skinless chicken breasts
- 60 g cream cheese, softened
- 55 g bacon bits
- 20 g chopped pickled jalapeños
- 40 g shredded Cheddar cheese, divided

Preparation Instructions :

1. Line the air fryer basket with parchment and spray lightly with oil.
2. Make multiple cuts across the top of each chicken breast, cutting only halfway through.
3. In a medium bowl, mix together the cream cheese, bacon bits, jalapeños, and Cheddar cheese. Spoon some of the mixture into each cut.
4. Place the chicken in the prepared basket.
5. Air fry at 176ºC for 14 minutes. Scatter the remaining cheese on top of the chicken and cook for another 2 to 5 minutes, or

until the cheese is melted and the internal temperature reaches 76°C.

Herbed Roast Chicken Breast

Prep time: 10 minutes/ Cook time: 25 minutes/ Serves 2 to 4

Ingredients :

- 2 tablespoons salted butter or ghee, at room temperature
- 1 teaspoon dried Italian seasoning, crushed
- ½ teaspoon kosher salt
- ½ teaspoon smoked paprika
- ¼ teaspoon black pepper
- 2 bone-in, skin-on chicken breast halves (280 g each)
- Lemon wedges, for serving

Preparation Instructions :

1. In a small bowl, stir together the butter, Italian seasoning, salt, paprika, and pepper until thoroughly combined.
2. Using a small sharp knife, carefully loosen the skin on each chicken breast half, starting at the thin end of each. Very carefully separate the skin from the flesh, leaving the skin attached at the thick end of each breast. Divide the herb butter into quarters. Rub one-quarter of the butter onto the flesh of each breast. Fold and lightly press the skin back onto each breast. Rub the remaining butter onto the skin of each breast.
3. Place the chicken in the air fryer basket. Set the air fryer to (190°C for 25 minutes. Use a meat thermometer to ensure the chicken breasts have reached an internal temperature of 76°C.
4. Transfer the chicken to a cutting board. Lightly cover with aluminum foil and let rest for 5 to 10 minutes.
5. Serve with lemon wedges.

Chicken Croquettes with Creole Sauce

Prep time: 30 minutes/ Cook time: 10 minutes/ Serves 4

Ingredients :

- 280 g shredded cooked chicken
- 120 g shredded Cheddar cheese
- 2 eggs
- 15 g finely chopped onion
- 25 g almond meal
- 1 tablespoon poultry seasoning
- Olive oil

Creole Sauce:
- 60 g mayonnaise
- 60 g sour cream
- 1½ teaspoons Dijon mustard
- 1½ teaspoons fresh lemon juice
- ½ teaspoon garlic powder
- ½ teaspoon Creole seasoning

Preparation Instructions :

1. In a large bowl, combine the chicken, Cheddar, eggs, onion, almond meal, and poultry seasoning. Stir gently until thoroughly combined. Cover and refrigerate for 30 minutes.
2. Meanwhile, to make the Creole sauce: In a small bowl, whisk together the mayonnaise, sour cream, Dijon mustard, lemon juice, garlic powder, and Creole seasoning until thoroughly combined. Cover and refrigerate until ready to serve.
3. Preheat the air fryer to 200°C. Divide the chicken mixture into 8 portions and shape into patties.
4. Working in batches if necessary, arrange the patties in a single layer in the air fryer basket and coat both sides lightly with olive oil. Pausing halfway through the cooking time to flip the patties, air fry

for 10 minutes, or until lightly browned and the cheese is melted. Serve with the Creole sauce.

Gochujang Chicken Wings

Prep time: 15 minutes/ Cook time: 25 minutes/ Serves 4

Ingredients :

Wings:
- 900 g chicken wings
- 1 teaspoon kosher salt
- 1 teaspoon black pepper or gochugaru (Korean red pepper)

Sauce:
- 2 tablespoons gochujang (Korean chili paste)
- 1 tablespoon mayonnaise
- 1 tablespoon toasted sesame oil
- 1 tablespoon minced fresh ginger
- 1 tablespoon minced garlic
- 1 teaspoon sugar
- 1 teaspoon agave nectar or honey
- For Serving
- 1 teaspoon sesame seeds
- 25 g chopped spring onions

Preparation Instructions :

1. For the wings: Season the wings with the salt and pepper and place in the air fryer basket. Set the air fryer to 200°C for 20 minutes, turning the wings halfway through the cooking time.
2. Meanwhile, for the sauce: In a small bowl, combine the gochujang, mayonnaise, sesame oil, ginger, garlic, sugar, and agave; set aside.
3. As you near the 20-minute mark, use a meat thermometer to check the meat. When the wings reach 70°C, transfer them to a large bowl. Pour about half the sauce on the wings; toss to coat (serve the remaining sauce as a dip).
4. Return the wings to the air fryer basket and cook for 5 minutes, until the sauce has glazed.
5. Transfer the wings to a serving platter. Sprinkle with the sesame seeds and spring onions. Serve with the reserved sauce on the side for dipping.

Piri-Piri Chicken Thighs

Prep time: 5 minutes/ Cook time: 25 minutes/ Serves 4

Ingredients :

- 60 ml piri-piri sauce
- 1 tablespoon freshly squeezed lemon juice
- 2 tablespoons brown sugar, divided
- 2 cloves garlic, minced
- 1 tablespoon extra-virgin olive oil
- 4 bone-in, skin-on chicken thighs, each weighing approximately 200 to 230 g
- ½ teaspoon cornflour

Preparation Instructions :

1. To make the marinade, whisk together the piri-piri sauce, lemon juice, 1 tablespoon of brown sugar, and the garlic in a small bowl. While whisking, slowly pour in the oil in a steady stream and continue to whisk until emulsified. Using a skewer, poke holes in the chicken thighs and place them in a small glass dish. Pour the marinade over the chicken and turn the thighs to coat them with the sauce. Cover the dish and refrigerate for at least 15 minutes and up to 1 hour.
2. Preheat the air fryer to 190°C. Remove the chicken thighs from the dish, reserving the marinade, and place them skin-side down in the air fryer basket. Air fry until the internal temperature reaches 76°C, 15 to 20 minutes.

3. Meanwhile, whisk the remaining brown sugar and the cornflour into the marinade and microwave it on high power for 1 minute until it is bubbling and thickened to a glaze.
4. Once the chicken is cooked, turn the thighs over and brush them with the glaze. Air fry for a few additional minutes until the glaze browns and begins to char in spots.
5. Remove the chicken to a platter and serve with additional piri-piri sauce, if desired.

Nacho Chicken Fries

Prep time: 20 minutes/ Cook time: 6 to 7 minutes per batch/ Serves 4 to 6

Ingredients :
- 450 g chicken tenders
- Salt, to taste
- 30 g flour
- 2 eggs
- 90 g panko bread crumbs
- 20 g crushed organic nacho cheese tortilla chips
- Oil for misting or cooking spray

Seasoning Mix:
- 1 tablespoon chili powder
- 1 teaspoon ground cumin
- ½ teaspoon garlic powder
- ½ teaspoon onion powder

Preparation Instructions :
1. Stir together all seasonings in a small cup and set aside.
2. Cut chicken tenders in half crosswise, then cut into strips no wider than about ½ inch.
3. Preheat the air fryer to 200°C.
4. Salt chicken to taste. Place strips in large bowl and sprinkle with 1 tablespoon of the seasoning mix. Stir well to distribute seasonings.
5. Add flour to chicken and stir well to coat all sides.
6. Beat eggs together in a shallow dish.
7. In a second shallow dish, combine the panko, crushed chips, and the remaining 2 teaspoons of seasoning mix.
8. Dip chicken strips in eggs, then roll in crumbs. Mist with oil or cooking spray.
9. Chicken strips will cook best if done in two batches. They can be crowded and overlapping a little but not stacked in double or triple layers.
10. Cook for 4 minutes. Shake basket, mist with oil, and cook 2 to 3 more minutes, until chicken juices run clear and outside is crispy.
11. Repeat step 10 to cook remaining chicken fries.

Cajun-Breaded Chicken Bites

Prep time: 10 minutes/ Cook time: 12 minutes/ Serves 4

Ingredients :
- 450 g boneless, skinless chicken breasts, cut into 1-inch cubes
- 120 g heavy whipping cream
- ½ teaspoon salt
- ¼ teaspoon ground black pepper
- 30 g plain pork rinds, finely crushed
- 40 g unflavoured whey protein powder
- ½ teaspoon Cajun seasoning

Preparation Instructions :
1. Place chicken in a medium bowl and pour in cream. Stir to coat. Sprinkle with salt and pepper.
2. In a separate large bowl, combine pork rinds, protein powder, and Cajun seasoning. Remove chicken from cream, shaking off any excess, and toss in dry

mix until fully coated.

3. Place bites into ungreased air fryer basket. Adjust the temperature to 200ºC and air fry for 12 minutes, shaking the basket twice during cooking. Bites will be done when golden brown and have an internal temperature of at least 76ºC. Serve warm.

Lemon Thyme Roasted Chicken

Prep time: 10 minutes/ Cook time: 60 minutes / Serves 6

Ingredients :

2 tablespoons baking powder
- 1 teaspoon smoked paprika
- Sea salt and freshly ground black pepper, to taste
- 900 g chicken wings or chicken drumettes
- Avocado oil spray
- 80 ml avocado oil
- 120 ml Buffalo hot sauce, such as Frank's RedHot
- 4 tablespoons unsalted butter
- 2 tablespoons apple cider vinegar
- 1 teaspoon minced garlic

Preparation Instructions :

1. In a large bowl, stir together the baking powder, smoked paprika, and salt and pepper to taste. Add the chicken wings and toss to coat.
2. Set the air fryer to 200ºC. Spray the wings with oil.
3. Place the wings in the basket in a single layer, working in batches, and air fry for 20 to 25 minutes. Check with an instant-read thermometer and remove when they reach 70ºC. Let rest until they reach 76ºC.
4. While the wings are cooking, whisk together the avocado oil, hot sauce, butter, vinegar, and garlic in a small saucepan over medium-low heat until warm.
5. When the wings are done cooking, toss them with the Buffalo sauce. Serve warm.

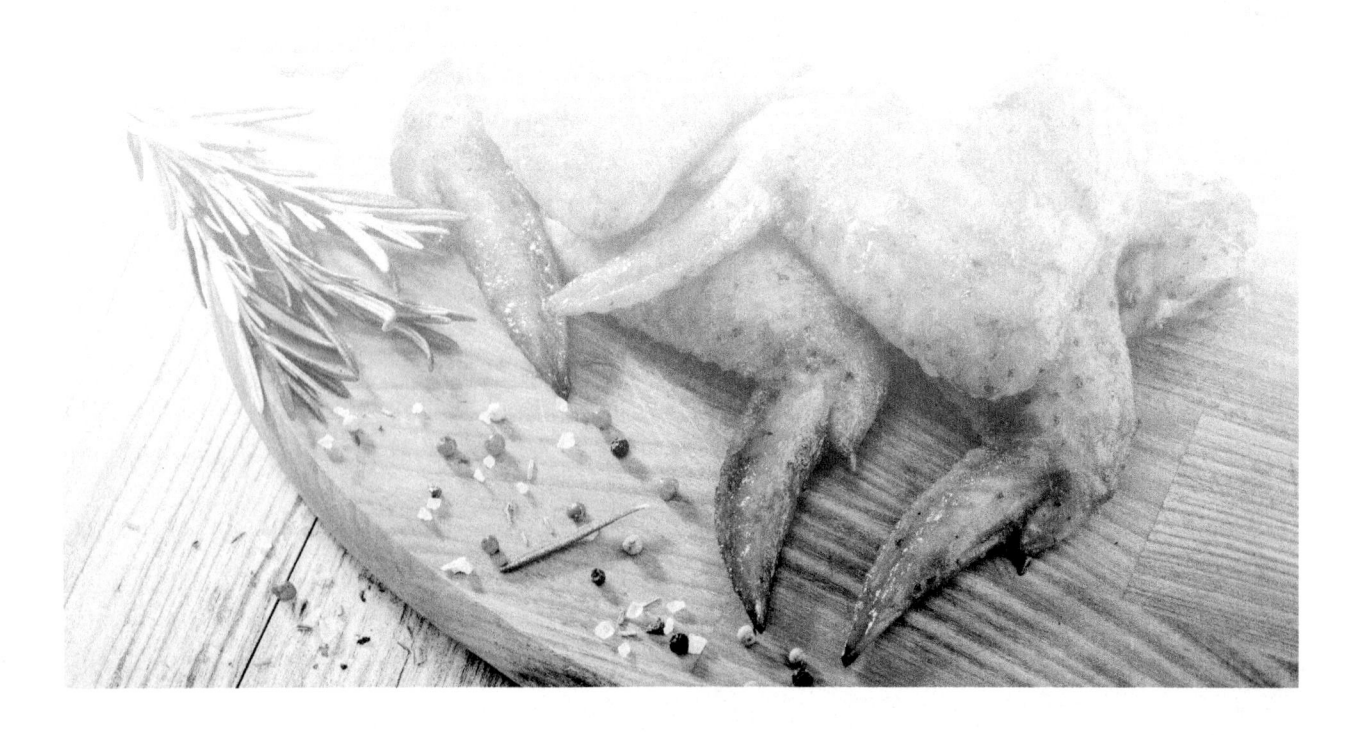

Chapter 4 Beef, Pork, and Lamb

Cantonese BBQ Pork

Prep time: 30 minutes/ Cook time: 15 minutes/ Serves 4

Ingredients :
- 60 ml honey
- 2 tablespoons dark soy sauce
- 1 tablespoon sugar
- 1 tablespoon Shaoxing wine (rice cooking wine)
- 1 tablespoon hoisin sauce
- 2 teaspoons minced garlic
- 2 teaspoons minced fresh ginger
- 1 teaspoon Chinese five-spice powder
- 450 g fatty pork shoulder, cut into long, 1-inch-thick pieces

Preparation Instructions :
1. In a small microwave-safe bowl, combine the honey, soy sauce, sugar, wine, hoisin, garlic, ginger, and five-spice powder. Microwave in 10-second intervals, stirring in between, until the honey has dissolved.
2. Use a fork to pierce the pork slices to allow the marinade to penetrate better. Place the pork in a large bowl or resealable plastic bag and pour in half the marinade; set aside the remaining marinade to use for the sauce. Toss to coat. Marinate the pork at room temperature for 30 minutes, or cover and refrigerate for up 24 hours.
3. Place the pork in a single layer in the air fryer basket. Set the air fryer to 204°C for 15 minutes, turning and basting the pork halfway through the cooking time.
4. While the pork is cooking, microwave the reserved marinade on high for 45 to 60 seconds, stirring every 15 seconds, to thicken it slightly to the consistency of a sauce.
5. Transfer the pork to a cutting board and let rest for 10 minutes. Brush with the sauce and serve.

Bacon-Wrapped Pork Tenderloin

Prep time: 30 minutes/ Cook time: 22 to 25 minutes /Serves 6

Ingredients :
- 120 ml minced onion
- 120 ml apple cider, or apple juice
- 60 ml honey
- 1 tablespoon minced garlic
- ¼ teaspoon salt
- ¼ teaspoon freshly ground black pepper
- 900 g pork tenderloin
- 1 to 2 tablespoons oil
- 8 uncooked bacon slices

Preparation Instructions :
1. In a medium bowl, stir together the onion, cider, honey, garlic, salt, and pepper. Transfer to a large resealable bag or airtight container and add the pork. Seal the bag. Refrigerate to marinate for at least 2 hours.
2. Preheat the air fryer to 204°C. Line the air fryer basket with parchment paper.
3. Remove the pork from the marinade and place it on the parchment. Spritz with oil.
4. Cook for 15 minutes.
5. Wrap the bacon slices around the pork and secure them with toothpicks. Turn the pork roast and spritz with oil. Cook

for 7 to 10 minutes more until the internal temperature reaches 64°C, depending on how well-done you like pork loin. It will continue cooking after it's removed from the fryer, so let it sit for 5 minutes before serving.

Cheese Crusted Chops

Prep time: 10 minutes/ Cook time: 12 minutes/ Serves 4 to 6

Ingredients :

- ¼ teaspoon pepper
- ½ teaspoons salt
- 4 to 6 thick boneless pork chops
- 235 ml pork scratching crumbs
- ¼ teaspoon chili powder
- ½ teaspoons onion granules
- 1 teaspoon smoked paprika
- 2 beaten eggs
- 3 tablespoons grated Parmesan cheese
- Cooking spray

Preparation Instructions :

1. Preheat the air fryer to 205°C.
2. Rub the pepper and salt on both sides of pork chops.
3. In a food processor, pulse pork scratchings into crumbs. Mix crumbs with chili powder, onion granules, and paprika in a bowl.
4. Beat eggs in another bowl.
5. Dip pork chops into eggs then into pork scratchings crumb mixture.
6. Spritz the air fryer basket with cooking spray and add pork chops to the basket.
7. Air fry for 12 minutes.
8. Serve garnished with the Parmesan cheese.

Kale and Beef Omelet

Prep time: 15 minutes/ Cook time: 16 minutes/ Serves 4

Ingredients :

- 230 g leftover beef, coarsely chopped
- 2 garlic cloves, pressed
- 235 ml kale, torn into pieces and wilted
- 1 tomato, chopped
- ¼ teaspoon sugar
- 4 eggs, beaten
- 4 tablespoons double cream
- ½ teaspoon turmeric powder
- Salt and ground black pepper, to taste
- ⅛ teaspoon ground allspice
- Cooking spray

Preparation Instructions :

1. Preheat the air fryer to 182°C. Spritz four ramekins with cooking spray.
2. Put equal amounts of each of the ingredients into each ramekin and mix well.
3. Air fry for 16 minutes. Serve immediately.

Vietnamese Grilled Pork

Prep time: 30 minutes/ Cook time: 20 minutes / Serves 6

Ingredients :

- 60 ml minced brown onion
- 2 tablespoons sugar
- 2 tablespoons vegetable oil
- 1 tablespoon minced garlic
- 1 tablespoon fish sauce
- 1 tablespoon minced fresh lemongrass
- 2 teaspoons dark soy sauce
- ½ teaspoon black pepper
- 680 g boneless pork shoulder, cut into ½-inch-thick slices
- 60 ml chopped salted roasted peanuts
- 2 tablespoons chopped fresh coriander or parsley

Preparation Instructions :

1. In a large bowl, combine the onion, sugar,

vegetable oil, garlic, fish sauce, lemongrass, soy sauce, and pepper. Add the pork and toss to coat. Marinate at room temperature for 30 minutes, or cover and refrigerate for up to 24 hours.
2. Arrange the pork slices in the air fryer basket; discard the marinade. Set the air fryer to 204°C for 20 minutes, turning the pork halfway through the cooking time.
3. Transfer the pork to a serving platter. Sprinkle with the peanuts and coriander and serve.

Sirloin Steak with Honey-Mustard Butter

Prep time: 5 minutes/ Cook time: 14 minutes/ Serves 4

Ingredients :
- 900 g beef sirloin steak
- 1 teaspoon cayenne pepper
- 1 tablespoon honey
- 1 tablespoon Dijon mustard
- ½ stick butter, softened
- Sea salt and freshly ground black pepper, to taste
- Cooking spray

Preparation Instructions :
1. Preheat the air fryer to 204°C and spritz with cooking spray.
2. Sprinkle the steak with cayenne pepper, salt, and black pepper on a clean work surface.
3. Arrange the steak in the preheated air fryer and spritz with cooking spray.
4. Air fry for 14 minutes or until browned and reach your desired doneness. Flip the steak halfway through.
5. Meanwhile, combine the honey, mustard, and butter in a small bowl. Stir to mix well.
6. Transfer the air fried steak onto a plate and baste with the honey-mustard butter before serving.

Lamb Burger with Feta and Olives

Prep time: 10 minutes/ Cook time: 20 minutes/ Serves 3 to 4

Ingredients :
- 2 teaspoons olive oil
- ⅓ onion, finely chopped
- 1 clove garlic, minced
- 450 g lamb mince
- 2 tablespoons fresh parsley, finely chopped
- 1½ teaspoons fresh oregano, finely chopped
- 120 ml black olives, finely chopped
- 80 ml crumbled feta cheese
- ½ teaspoon salt
- Freshly ground black pepper, to taste
- 4 thick pitta breads

Preparation Instructions :
1. Preheat a medium skillet over medium-high heat on the stovetop. Add the olive oil and cook the onion until tender, but not browned, about 4 to 5 minutes. Add the garlic and cook for another minute. Transfer the onion and garlic to a mixing bowl and add the lamb mince, parsley, oregano, olives, feta cheese, salt and pepper. Gently mix the ingredients together.
2. Divide the mixture into 3 or 4 equal portions and then form the hamburgers, being careful not to over-handle the meat. One good way to do this is to throw the meat back and forth between your hands like a baseball, packing the meat each time you catch it. Flatten the balls into patties, making an indentation in the center of each patty. Flatten the sides of

the patties as well to make it easier to fit them into the air fryer basket.
3. Preheat the air fryer to 188°C.
4. If you don't have room for all four burgers, air fry two or three burgers at a time for 8 minutes at 188°C. Flip the burgers over and air fry for another 8 minutes. If you cooked your burgers in batches, return the first batch of burgers to the air fryer for the last two minutes of cooking to re-heat. This should give you a medium-well burger. If you'd prefer a medium-rare burger, shorten the cooking time to about 13 minutes. Remove the burgers to a resting plate and let the burgers rest for a few minutes before dressing and serving.
5. While the burgers are resting, toast the pitta breads in the air fryer for 2 minutes. Tuck the burgers into the toasted pitta breads, or wrap the pittas around the burgers and serve with a tzatziki sauce or some mayonnaise.

Short Ribs with Chimichurri

Prep time: 30 minutes/ Cook time: 13 minutes/ Serves 4

Ingredients :
- 450 g boneless short ribs
- 1½ teaspoons sea salt, divided
- ½ teaspoon freshly ground black pepper, divided
- 120 ml fresh parsley leaves
- 120 ml fresh coriander leaves
- 1 teaspoon minced garlic
- 1 tablespoon freshly squeezed lemon juice
- ½ teaspoon ground cumin
- ¼ teaspoon red pepper flakes
- 2 tablespoons extra-virgin olive oil
- Avocado oil spray

Preparation Instructions :
1. Pat the short ribs dry with paper towels. Sprinkle the ribs all over with 1 teaspoon salt and ¼ teaspoon black pepper. Let sit at room temperature for 45 minutes.
2. Meanwhile, place the parsley, coriander, garlic, lemon juice, cumin, red pepper flakes, the remaining ½ teaspoon salt, and the remaining ¼ teaspoon black pepper in a blender or food processor. With the blender running, slowly drizzle in the olive oil. Blend for about 1 minute, until the mixture is smooth and well combined.
3. Set the air fryer to 204°C. Spray both sides of the ribs with oil. Place in the basket and air fry for 8 minutes. Flip and cook for another 5 minutes, until an instant-read thermometer reads 52°C for medium-rare (or to your desired doneness).
4. Allow the meat to rest for 5 to 10 minutes, then slice. Serve warm with the chimichurri sauce.

Italian Sausage Links

Prep time: 10 minutes/ Cook time: 24 minutes/ Serves 4

Ingredients :
- 1 pepper (any color), sliced
- 1 medium onion, sliced
- 1 tablespoon avocado oil
- 1 teaspoon Italian seasoning
- Sea salt and freshly ground black pepper, to taste
- 450 g Italian-seasoned sausage links

Preparation Instructions :
1. Place the pepper and onion in a medium bowl, and toss with the avocado oil, Italian seasoning, and salt and pepper to taste.

2. Set the air fryer to 204°C. Put the vegetables in the air fryer basket and cook for 12 minutes.
3. Push the vegetables to the side of the basket and arrange the sausage links in the bottom of the basket in a single layer. Spoon the vegetables over the sausages. Cook for 12 minutes, tossing halfway through, until an instant-read thermometer inserted into the sausage reads 72°C.

Minute Steak Roll-Ups

Prep time: 30 minutes/ Cook time: 8 to 10 minutes/ Serves 4

Ingredients :
- 4 minute steaks (170 g each)
- 1 (450 g) bottle Italian dressing
- 1 teaspoon salt
- ½ teaspoon freshly ground black pepper
- 120 ml finely chopped brown onion
- 120 ml finely chopped green pepper
- 120 ml finely chopped mushrooms
- 1 to 2 tablespoons oil

Preparation Instructions :
1. In a large resealable bag or airtight storage container, combine the steaks and Italian dressing. Seal the bag and refrigerate to marinate for 2 hours.
2. Remove the steaks from the marinade and place them on a cutting board. Discard the marinade. Evenly season the steaks with salt and pepper.
3. In a small bowl, stir together the onion, pepper, and mushrooms. Sprinkle the onion mixture evenly over the steaks. Roll up the steaks, jelly roll-style, and secure with toothpicks.
4. Preheat the air fryer to 204°C.
5. Place the steaks in the air fryer basket.
6. Cook for 4 minutes. Flip the steaks and spritz them with oil. Cook for 4 to 6 minutes more until the internal temperature reaches 64°C. Let rest for 5 minutes before serving.

Herb-Crusted Lamb Chops

Prep time: 10 minutes/ Cook time: 5 minutes/ Serves 2

Ingredients :
- 1 large egg
- 2 cloves garlic, minced
- 60 ml finely crushed pork scratchings
- 60 ml pre-grated Parmesan cheese
- 1 tablespoon chopped fresh oregano leaves
- 1 tablespoon chopped fresh rosemary leaves
- 1 teaspoon chopped fresh thyme leaves
- ½ teaspoon ground black pepper
- 4 (1-inch-thick) lamb chops

For Garnish/Serving (Optional):
- Sprigs of fresh oregano
- Sprigs of fresh rosemary
- Sprigs of fresh thyme
- Lavender flowers
- Lemon slices

Preparation Instructions :
1. Spray the air fryer basket with avocado oil. Preheat the air fryer to 204°C.
2. Beat the egg in a shallow bowl, add the garlic, and stir well to combine. In another shallow bowl, mix together the crushed pork scratchings, Parmesan, herbs, and pepper.
3. One at a time, dip the lamb chops into the egg mixture, shake off the excess egg, and then dredge them in the Parmesan mixture. Use your hands to coat the chops well in the Parmesan mixture and form a nice crust on all sides; if necessary, dip the chops again in both the egg and the

Parmesan mixture.

4. Place the lamb chops in the air fryer basket, leaving space between them, and air fry for 5 minutes, or until the internal temperature reaches 64°C for medium doneness. Allow to rest for 10 minutes before serving.
5. Garnish with sprigs of oregano, rosemary, and thyme, and lavender flowers, if desired. Serve with lemon slices, if desired.
6. Best served fresh. Store leftovers in an airtight container in the fridge for up to 4 days. Serve chilled over a salad, or reheat in a 176°C air fryer for 3 minutes, or until heated through.

Garlic Butter Steak Bites

Prep time: 5 minutes/ Cook time: 16 minutes/ Serves 3

Ingredients :
- Oil, for spraying
- 450 g boneless steak, cut into 1-inch pieces
- 2 tablespoons olive oil
- 1 teaspoon Worcestershire sauce
- ½ teaspoon granulated garlic
- ½ teaspoon salt
- ¼ teaspoon freshly ground black pepper

Preparation Instructions :
1. Preheat the air fryer to 204°C. Line the air fryer basket with parchment and spray lightly with oil.
2. In a medium bowl, combine the steak, olive oil, Worcestershire sauce, garlic, salt, and black pepper and toss until evenly coated.
3. Place the steak in a single layer in the prepared basket. You may have to work in batches, depending on the size of your air fryer.
4. Cook for 10 to 16 minutes, flipping every 3 to 4 minutes. The total cooking time will depend on the thickness of the meat and your preferred doneness. If you want it well done, it may take up to 5 additional minutes.

Kheema Meatloaf

Prep time: 10 minutes/ Cook time: 15 minutes/ Serves 4

Ingredients :
- 450 g 85% lean beef mince
- 2 large eggs, lightly beaten
- 235 ml diced brown onion
- 60 ml chopped fresh coriander
- 1 tablespoon minced fresh ginger
- 1 tablespoon minced garlic
- 2 teaspoons garam masala
- 1 teaspoon coarse or flaky salt
- 1 teaspoon ground turmeric
- 1 teaspoon cayenne pepper
- ½ teaspoon ground cinnamon
- ⅛ teaspoon ground cardamom

Preparation Instructions :
1. In a large bowl, gently mix the beef mince, eggs, onion, coriander, ginger, garlic, garam masala, salt, turmeric, cayenne, cinnamon, and cardamom until thoroughly combined.
2. Place the seasoned meat in a baking pan. Place the pan in the air fryer basket. Set the air fryer to 176°C for 15 minutes. Use a meat thermometer to ensure the meat loaf has reached an internal temperature of 72°C (medium).
3. Drain the fat and liquid from the pan and let stand for 5 minutes before slicing.
4. Slice and serve hot.

Filipino Crispy Pork Belly

Prep time: 20 minutes/ Cook time: 30 minutes/

Serves 4

Ingredients :
- 450 g pork belly
- 700 ml water
- 6 garlic cloves
- 2 tablespoons soy sauce
- 1 teaspoon coarse or flaky salt
- 1 teaspoon black pepper
- 2 bay leaves

Preparation Instructions :
1. Cut the pork belly into three thick chunks so it will cook more evenly.
2. Place the pork, water, garlic, soy sauce, salt, pepper, and bay leaves in the inner pot of an Instant Pot or other electric pressure cooker. Seal and cook at high pressure for 15 minutes. Let the pressure release naturally for 10 minutes, then manually release the remaining pressure. (If you do not have a pressure cooker, place all the ingredients in a large saucepan. Cover and cook over low heat until a knife can be easily inserted into the skin side of pork belly, about 1 hour.) Using tongs, very carefully transfer the meat to a wire rack over a rimmed baking sheet to drain and dry for 10 minutes.
3. Cut each chunk of pork belly into two long slices. Arrange the slices in the air fryer basket. Set the air fryer to 204°C for 15 minutes, or until the fat has crisped.
4. Serve immediately.

Apple Cornbread Stuffed Pork Loin

Prep time: 15 minutes/ Cook time: 1 hour/ Serves 4 to 6

Ingredients :
- 4 strips of bacon, chopped
- 1 Granny Smith apple, peeled, cored and finely chopped
- 2 teaspoons fresh thyme leaves
- 60 ml chopped fresh parsley
- 475 ml cubed cornbread
- 120 ml chicken stock
- Salt and freshly ground black pepper, to taste
- 1 (900 g) boneless pork loin

Apple Gravy:
- 2 tablespoons butter
- 1 shallot, minced
- 1 Granny Smith apple, peeled, cored and finely chopped
- 3 sprigs fresh thyme
- 2 tablespoons flour
- 235 ml chicken stock
- 120 ml apple cider
- Salt and freshly ground black pepper, to taste

Preparation Instructions :
1. Preheat the air fryer to 204°C.
2. Add the bacon to the air fryer and air fry for 6 to 8 minutes until crispy. While the bacon is cooking, combine the apple, fresh thyme, parsley and cornbread in a bowl and toss well. Moisten the mixture with the chicken stock and season to taste with salt and freshly ground black pepper. Add the cooked bacon to the mixture.
3. Butterfly the pork loin by holding it flat on the cutting board with one hand, while slicing into the pork loin parallel to the cutting board with the other. Slice into the longest side of the pork loin, but stop before you cut all the way through. You should then be able to open the pork loin up like a book, making it twice as wide as it was when you started. Season the inside of the pork with salt and freshly ground black pepper.
4. Spread the cornbread mixture onto the butterflied pork loin, leaving a one-inch

border around the edge of the pork. Roll the pork loin up around the stuffing to enclose the stuffing, and tie the rolled pork in several places with kitchen twine or secure with toothpicks. Try to replace any stuffing that falls out of the roast as you roll it, by stuffing it into the ends of the rolled pork. Season the outside of the pork with salt and freshly ground black pepper.
5. Preheat the air fryer to 182°C.
6. Place the stuffed pork loin into the air fryer, seam side down. Air fry the pork loin for 15 minutes at 182°C. Turn the pork loin over and air fry for an additional 15 minutes. Turn the pork loin a quarter turn and air fry for an additional 15 minutes. Turn the pork loin over again to expose the fourth side, and air fry for an additional 10 minutes. The pork loin should register 68°C on an instant read thermometer when it is finished.
7. While the pork is cooking, make the apple gravy. Preheat a saucepan over medium heat on the stovetop and melt the butter. Add the shallot, apple and thyme sprigs and sauté until the apple starts to soften and brown a little. Add the flour and stir for a minute or two. Whisk in the stock and apple cider vigorously to prevent the flour from forming lumps. Bring the mixture to a boil to thicken and season to taste with salt and pepper.
8. Transfer the pork loin to a resting plate and loosely tent with foil, letting the pork rest for at least 5 minutes before slicing and serving with the apple gravy poured over the top.

Bulgogi Burgers

Prep time: 30 minutes/ Cook time: 10 minutes/ Serves 4

Ingredients :
Burgers:
- 450 g 85% lean beef mince
- 60 ml chopped spring onionspring onions
- 2 tablespoons gochujang (Korean red chili paste)
- 1 tablespoon dark soy sauce
- 2 teaspoons minced garlic
- 2 teaspoons minced fresh ginger
- 2 teaspoons sugar
- 1 tablespoon toasted sesame oil
- ½ teaspoon coarse or flaky salt

Gochujang Mayonnaise:
- 60 ml mayonnaise
- 60 ml chopped spring onionspring onions
- 1 tablespoon gochujang (Korean red chili paste)• 1 tablespoon toasted sesame oil
- 2 teaspoons sesame seeds
- 4 hamburger buns

Preparation Instructions :
1. For the burgers: In a large bowl, mix the ground beef, spring onionspring onions, gochujang, soy sauce, garlic, ginger, sugar, sesame oil, and salt. Marinate at room temperature for 30 minutes, or cover and refrigerate for up to 24 hours.
2. Divide the meat into four portions and form them into round patties. Make a slight depression in the middle of each patty with your thumb to prevent them from puffing up into a dome shape while cooking.
3. Place the patties in a single layer in the air fryer basket. Set the air fryer to 176°C for 10 minutes.
4. Meanwhile, for the gochujang mayonnaise: Stir together the mayonnaise, spring onionspring onions, gochujang, sesame oil, and sesame seeds.
5. At the end of the cooking time, use a meat thermometer to ensure the burgers have

reached an internal temperature of 72°C (medium).
6. To serve, place the burgers on the buns and top with the mayonnaise.

Fajita Meatball Lettuce Wraps

Prep time: 10 minutes/ Cook time: 10 minutes/ Serves 4

Ingredients :

- 450 g beef mince (85% lean)
- 120 ml salsa, plus more for serving if desired
- 60 ml chopped onions
- 60 ml diced green or red peppers
- 1 large egg, beaten
- 1 teaspoon fine sea salt
- ½ teaspoon chili powder
- ½ teaspoon ground cumin
- 1 clove garlic, minced

For Serving (Optional):
- 8 leaves butterhead lettuce
- Pico de gallo or salsa
- Lime slices

Preparation Instructions :

1. Spray the air fryer basket with avocado oil. Preheat the air fryer to 176°C.
2. In a large bowl, mix together all the ingredients until well combined.
3. Shape the meat mixture into eight 1-inch balls. Place the meatballs in the air fryer basket, leaving a little space between them. Air fry for 10 minutes, or until cooked through and no longer pink inside and the internal temperature reaches 64°C.
4. Serve each meatball on a lettuce leaf, topped with pico de gallo or salsa, if desired. Serve with lime slices if desired.
5. Store leftovers in an airtight container in the fridge for 3 days or in the freezer for up to a month. Reheat in a preheated 176°C air fryer for 4 minutes, or until heated through.

Barbecue Ribs

Prep time: 5 minutes/ Cook time: 30 minutes/ Serves 4

Ingredients :

- 1 (900 g) rack baby back ribs
- 1 teaspoon onion granules
- 1 teaspoon garlic powder
- 1 teaspoon light brown sugar
- 1 teaspoon dried oregano
- Salt and freshly ground black pepper, to taste
- Cooking oil spray
- 120 ml barbecue sauce

Preparation Instructions :

1. Use a sharp knife to remove the thin membrane from the back of the ribs. Cut the rack in half, or as needed, so the ribs fit in the air fryer basket. The best way to do this is to cut the ribs into 4- or 5-rib sections.
2. In a small bowl, stir together the onion granules, garlic powder, brown sugar, and oregano and season with salt and pepper. Rub the spice seasoning onto the front and back of the ribs.
3. Cover the ribs with plastic wrap or foil and let sit at room temperature for 30 minutes.
4. Insert the crisper plate into the basket and the basket into the unit. Preheat the unit by selecting AIR ROAST, setting the temperature to 182°C, and setting the time to 3 minutes. Select START/STOP to begin.
5. Once the unit is preheated, spray the crisper plate with cooking oil. Place the ribs into the basket. It is okay to stack

them.
6. Select AIR ROAST, set the temperature to 182ºC, and set the time to 30 minutes. Select START/STOP to begin.
7. After 15 minutes, flip the ribs. Resume cooking for 15 minutes, or until a food thermometer registers 88ºC.
8. When the cooking is complete, transfer the ribs to a serving dish. Drizzle the ribs with the barbecue sauce and serve.

Ritzy Skirt Steak Fajitas

Prep time: 15 minutes/ Cook time: 30 minutes/ Serves 4

Ingredients :
- 2 tablespoons olive oil
- 60 ml lime juice
- 1 clove garlic, minced
- ½ teaspoon ground cumin
- ½ teaspoon hot sauce
- ½ teaspoon salt
- 2 tablespoons chopped fresh coriander
- 450 g skirt steak
- 1 onion, sliced
- 1 teaspoon chili powder
- 1 red pepper, sliced
- 1 green pepper, sliced
- Salt and freshly ground black pepper, to taste
- 8 flour tortillas

Toppings:
- Shredded lettuce
- Crumbled feta or ricotta (or grated Cheddar cheese)
- Sliced black olives
- Diced tomatoes
- Sour cream
- Guacamole

Preparation Instructions :
1. Combine the olive oil, lime juice, garlic, cumin, hot sauce, salt and coriander in a shallow dish. Add the skirt steak and turn it over several times to coat all sides. Pierce the steak with a needle-style meat tenderizer or paring knife. Marinate the steak in the refrigerator for at least 3 hours, or overnight. When you are ready to cook, remove the steak from the refrigerator and let it sit at room temperature for 30 minutes.
2. Preheat the air fryer to 204ºC.
3. Toss the onion slices with the chili powder and a little olive oil and transfer them to the air fryer basket. Air fry for 5 minutes. Add the red and green peppers to the air fryer basket with the onions, season with salt and pepper and air fry for 8 more minutes, until the onions and peppers are soft. Transfer the vegetables to a dish and cover with aluminum foil to keep warm.
4. Put the skirt steak in the air fryer basket and pour the marinade over the top. Air fry at 204ºC for 12 minutes. Flip the steak over and air fry for an additional 5 minutes. Transfer the cooked steak to a cutting board and let the steak rest for a few minutes. If the peppers and onions need to be heated, return them to the air fryer for just 1 to 2 minutes.
5. Thinly slice the steak at an angle, cutting against the grain of the steak. Serve the steak with the onions and peppers, the warm tortillas and the fajita toppings on the side.

Caraway Crusted Beef Steaks

Prep time: 5 minutes/ Cook time: 10 minutes/ Serves 4

Ingredients :
- 4 beef steaks

- 2 teaspoons caraway seeds
- 2 teaspoons garlic powder
- Sea salt and cayenne pepper, to taste
- 1 tablespoon melted butter
- 80 ml almond flour
- 2 eggs, beaten

Preparation Instructions :

1. Preheat the air fryer to 179°C.
2. Add the beef steaks to a large bowl and toss with the caraway seeds, garlic powder, salt and pepper until well coated.
3. Stir together the melted butter and almond flour in a bowl. Whisk the eggs in a different bowl.
4. Dredge the seasoned steaks in the eggs, then dip in the almond and butter mixture.
5. Arrange the coated steaks in the air fryer basket. Air fryer for 10 minutes, or until the internal temperature of the beef steaks reaches at least 64°C on a meat thermometer. Flip the steaks once halfway through to ensure even cooking.
6. Transfer the steaks to plates. Let cool for 5 minutes and serve hot.

Pork Milanese

Prep time: 10 minutes/ Cook time: 12 minutes/ Serves 4

Ingredients :

- 4 (1-inch) boneless pork chops
- Fine sea salt and ground black pepper, to taste
- 2 large eggs
- 180 ml pre-grated Parmesan cheese
- Chopped fresh parsley, for garnish
- Lemon slices, for serving

Preparation Instructions :

1. Spray the air fryer basket with avocado oil. Preheat the air fryer to 204°C.
2. Place the pork chops between 2 sheets of plastic wrap and pound them with the flat side of a meat tenderizer until they're ¼ inch thick. Lightly season both sides of the chops with salt and pepper.
3. Lightly beat the eggs in a shallow bowl. Divide the Parmesan cheese evenly between 2 bowls and set the bowls in this order: Parmesan, eggs, Parmesan. Dredge a chop in the first bowl of Parmesan, then dip it in the eggs, and then dredge it again in the second bowl of Parmesan, making sure both sides and all edges are well coated. Repeat with the remaining chops.
4. Place the chops in the air fryer basket and air fry for 12 minutes, or until the internal temperature reaches 64°C, flipping halfway through.
5. Garnish with fresh parsley and serve immediately with lemon slices. Store leftovers in an airtight container in the refrigerator for up to 3 days. Reheat in a preheated 200°C air fryer for 5 minutes, or until warmed through.

Pork Schnitzels with Sour Cream and Dill Sauce

Prep time: 5 minutes/ Cook time: 24 minutes/ Serves 4 to 6

Ingredients :

- 120 ml flour
- 1½ teaspoons salt
- Freshly ground black pepper, to taste
- 2 eggs
- 120 ml milk
- 355 ml toasted breadcrumbs
- 1 teaspoon paprika
- 6 boneless pork chops (about 680 g), fat trimmed, pound to ½-inch thick
- 2 tablespoons olive oil
- 3 tablespoons melted butter

- Lemon wedges, for serving

Sour Cream and Dill Sauce:
- 235 ml chicken stock
- 1½ tablespoons cornflour
- 80 ml sour cream
- 1½ tablespoons chopped fresh dill
- Salt and ground black pepper, to taste

Preparation Instructions :

1. Preheat the air fryer to 204ºC.
2. Combine the flour with salt and black pepper in a large bowl. Stir to mix well. Whisk the egg with milk in a second bowl. Stir the breadcrumbs and paprika in a third bowl.
3. Dredge the pork chops in the flour bowl, then in the egg milk, and then into the breadcrumbs bowl. Press to coat well. Shake the excess off.
4. Arrange one pork chop in the preheated air fryer each time, then brush with olive oil and butter on all sides.
5. Air fry each pork chop for 4 minutes or until golden brown and crispy. Flip the chop halfway through the cooking time.
6. Transfer the cooked pork chop (schnitzel) to a baking pan in the oven and keep warm over low heat while air frying the remaining pork chops.
7. Meanwhile, combine the chicken stock and cornflour in a small saucepan and bring to a boil over medium-high heat. Simmer for 2 more minutes.
8. Turn off the heat, then mix in the sour cream, fresh dill, salt, and black pepper.
9. Remove the schnitzels from the air fryer to a plate and baste with sour cream and dill sauce. Squeeze the lemon wedges over and slice to serve.

Sausage-Stuffed Peppers

Prep time: 15 minutes/ Cook time: 28 to 30 minutes /Serves 6

Ingredients :Avocado oil spray

- 230 g Italian-seasoned sausage, casings removed
- 120 ml chopped mushrooms
- 60 ml diced onion
- 1 teaspoon Italian seasoning
- Sea salt and freshly ground black pepper, to taste
- 235 ml keto-friendly marinara sauce
- 3 peppers, halved and seeded
- 85 g low-moisture Mozzarella or other melting cheese, shredded

Preparation Instructions :

1. Spray a large skillet with oil and place it over medium-high heat. Add the sausage and cook for 5 minutes, breaking up the meat with a wooden spoon. Add the mushrooms, onion, and Italian seasoning, and season with salt and pepper. Cook for 5 minutes more. Stir in the marinara sauce and cook until heated through.
2. Scoop the sausage filling into the pepper halves.
3. Set the air fryer to 176ºC. Arrange the peppers in a single layer in the air fryer basket, working in batches if necessary. Air fry for 15 minutes.
4. Top the stuffed peppers with the cheese and air fry for 3 to 5 minutes more, until the cheese is melted and the peppers are tender.

Sausage and Cauliflower Arancini

Prep time: 30 minutes/ Cook time: 28 to 32 minutes /Serves 6

Ingredients :
- Avocado oil spray
- 170 g Italian-seasoned sausage, casings removed
- 60 ml diced onion
- 1 teaspoon minced garlic
- 1 teaspoon dried thyme
- Sea salt and freshly ground black pepper, to taste
- 120 ml cauliflower rice
- 85 g cream cheese
- 110 g Cheddar cheese, shredded
- 1 large egg
- 120 ml finely ground blanched almond flour
- 60 ml finely grated Parmesan cheese
- Keto-friendly marinara sauce, for serving

Preparation Instructions :
1. Spray a large skillet with oil and place it over medium-high heat. Once the skillet is hot, put the sausage in the skillet and cook for 7 minutes, breaking up the meat with the back of a spoon.
2. Reduce the heat to medium and add the onion. Cook for 5 minutes, then add the garlic, thyme, and salt and pepper to taste. Cook for 1 minute more.
3. Add the cauliflower rice and cream cheese to the skillet. Cook for 7 minutes, stirring frequently, until the cream cheese melts and the cauliflower is tender.
4. Remove the skillet from the heat and stir in the Cheddar cheese. Using a cookie scoop, form the mixture into 1½-inch balls. Place the balls on a parchment paper-lined baking sheet. Freeze for 30 minutes.
5. Place the egg in a shallow bowl and beat it with a fork. In a separate bowl, stir together the almond flour and Parmesan cheese.
6. Dip the cauliflower balls into the egg, then coat them with the almond flour mixture, gently pressing the mixture to the balls to adhere.
7. Set the air fryer to 204ºC. Spray the cauliflower rice balls with oil, and arrange them in a single layer in the air fryer basket, working in batches if necessary. Air fry for 5 minutes. Flip the rice balls and spray them with more oil. Air fry for 3 to 7 minutes longer, until the balls are golden brown.
8. Serve warm with marinara sauce.

Herbed Lamb Steaks

Prep time: 30 minutes/ Cook time: 15 minutes/ Serves 4

Ingredients :
- ½ medium onion
- 2 tablespoons minced garlic
- 2 teaspoons ground ginger
- 1 teaspoon ground cinnamon
- 1 teaspoon onion granules
- 1 teaspoon cayenne pepper
- 1 teaspoon salt
- 4 (170 g) boneless lamb sirloin steaks
- Oil, for spraying

Preparation Instructions :
1. In a blender, combine the onion, garlic, ginger, cinnamon, onion granules, cayenne pepper, and salt and pulse until the onion is minced.
2. Place the lamb steaks in a large bowl or zip-top plastic bag and sprinkle the onion mixture over the top. Turn the steaks until they are evenly coated. Cover with plastic wrap or seal the bag and refrigerate for 30 minutes.
3. Preheat the air fryer to 164ºC. Line the air fryer basket with parchment and spray

lightly with oil.
4. Place the lamb steaks in a single layer in the prepared basket, making sure they don't overlap. You may need to work in batches, depending on the size of your air fryer.
5. Cook for 8 minutes, flip, and cook for another 7 minutes, or until the internal temperature reaches 68°C.

Chicken Fried Steak with Cream Gravy

Prep time: 5 minutes/ Cook time: 10 minutes/ Serves 4

Ingredients :
- 4 small thin minute steaks (about 450 g)
- ½ teaspoon salt
- ½ teaspoon freshly ground black pepper
- ¼ teaspoon garlic powder
- 1 egg, lightly beaten
- 235 ml crushed pork scratchings (about 85 g)

Cream Gravy:
- 120 ml double cream
- 60 g cream cheese
- 60 ml bacon fat
- 2 to 3 tablespoons water
- 2 to 3 dashes Worcestershire sauce
- Salt and freshly ground black pepper, to taste

Preparation Instructions :
1. Preheat the air fryer to 204°C.
2. Working one at a time, place the steak between two sheets of parchment paper and use a meat mallet to pound to an even thickness.
3. In a small bowl, combine the salt, pepper, and garlic power. Season both sides of each steak with the mixture.
4. Place the egg in a small shallow dish and the pork rinds in another small shallow dish. Dip each steak first in the egg wash, followed by the pork scratchings, pressing lightly to form an even coating. Working in batches if necessary, arrange the steaks in a single layer in the air fryer basket. Air fry for 10 minutes until crispy and cooked through.
5. To make the cream gravy: In a heavy-bottomed pot, warm the cream, cream cheese, and bacon fat over medium heat, whisking until smooth. Lower the heat if the mixture begins to boil. Continue whisking as you slowly add the water, 1 tablespoon at a time, until the sauce reaches the desired consistency. Season with the Worcestershire sauce and salt and pepper to taste. Serve over the chicken fried steaks.

Parmesan-Crusted Pork Chops

Prep time: 5 minutes/ Cook time: 12 minutes/ Serves 4

Ingredients :
- 1 large egg
- 120 ml grated Parmesan cheese
- 4 (110 g) boneless pork chops
- ½ teaspoon salt
- ¼ teaspoon ground black pepper

Preparation Instructions :
1. Whisk egg in a medium bowl and place Parmesan in a separate medium bowl.
2. Sprinkle pork chops on both sides with salt and pepper. Dip each pork chop into egg, then press both sides into Parmesan.
3. Place pork chops into ungreased air fryer basket. Adjust the temperature to

204ºC and air fry for 12 minutes, turning chops halfway through cooking. Pork chops will be golden and have an internal temperature of at least 64ºC when done. Serve warm.

Bo Luc Lac

Prep time: 50 minutes/ Cook time: 8 minutes/ Serves 4

Ingredients :

For the Meat:
- 2 teaspoons soy sauce
- 4 garlic cloves, minced
- 1 teaspoon coarse or flaky salt
- 2 teaspoons sugar
- ¼ teaspoon ground black pepper
- 1 teaspoon toasted sesame oil
- 680 g top rump steak, cut into 1-inch cubes
- Cooking spray

For the Salad:
- 1 head butterhead lettuce, leaves separated and torn into large pieces
- 60 ml fresh mint leaves
- 120 ml halved baby plum tomatoes
- ½ red onion, halved and thinly sliced
- 2 tablespoons apple cider vinegar
- 1 garlic clove, minced
- 2 teaspoons sugar
- ¼ teaspoon coarse or flaky salt
- ¼ teaspoon ground black pepper
- 2 tablespoons vegetable oil

For Serving:
- Lime wedges, for garnish
- Coarse salt and freshly cracked black pepper, to taste

Preparation Instructions :

1. Combine the ingredients for the meat, except for the steak, in a large bowl. Stir to mix well.
2. Dunk the steak cubes in the bowl and press to coat. Wrap the bowl in plastic and marinate under room temperature for at least 30 minutes.
3. Preheat the air fryer to 232ºC. Spritz the air fryer basket with cooking spray.
4. Discard the marinade and transfer the steak cubes in the preheated air fryer basket. You need to air fry in batches to avoid overcrowding.
5. Air fry for 4 minutes or until the steak cubes are lightly browned but still have a little pink. Shake the basket halfway through the cooking time.
6. Meanwhile, combine the ingredients for the salad in a separate large bowl. Toss to mix well.
7. Pour the salad in a large serving bowl and top with the steak cubes. Squeeze the lime wedges over and sprinkle with salt and black pepper before serving.

Kielbasa and Cabbage

Prep time: 10 minutes/ Cook time: 20 to 25 minutes/ Serves 4

Ingredients :

- 450 g smoked kielbasa sausage, sliced into ½-inch pieces
- 1 head cabbage, very coarsely chopped
- ½ brown onion, chopped
- 2 cloves garlic, chopped
- 2 tablespoons olive oil
- ½ teaspoon salt
- ½ teaspoon freshly ground black pepper
- 60 ml water

Preparation Instructions :

1. Preheat the air fryer to 204ºC.
2. In a large bowl, combine the sausage, cabbage, onion, garlic, olive oil, salt, and black pepper. Toss until thoroughly combined.

3. Transfer the mixture to the basket of the air fryer and pour the water over the top. Pausing two or three times during the cooking time to shake the basket, air fry for 20 to 25 minutes, until the sausage is browned and the vegetables are tender.

Bacon and Cheese Stuffed Pork Chops

Prep time: 10 minutes/ Cook time: 12 minutes/ Serves 4

Ingredients :

- 15 g plain pork scratchings, finely crushed
- 120 ml shredded sharp Cheddar cheese
- 4 slices cooked bacon, crumbled
- 4 (110 g) boneless pork chops
- ½ teaspoon salt
- ¼ teaspoon ground black pepper

Preparation Instructions :

1. In a small bowl, mix pork scratchings, Cheddar, and bacon.
2. Make a 3-inch slit in the side of each pork chop and stuff with ¼ pork rind mixture. Sprinkle each side of pork chops with salt and pepper.
3. Place pork chops into ungreased air fryer basket, stuffed side up. Adjust the temperature to 204°C and air fry for 12 minutes. Pork chops will be browned and have an internal temperature of at least 64°C when done. Serve warm.

Chapter 5 Fish and Seafood

Stuffed Sole Florentine

Prep time: 10 minutes/ Cook time: 25 minutes/ Serves 4

Ingredients :
- 40 g pine nuts
- 2 tablespoons olive oil
- 90 g chopped tomatoes
- 170 g bag spinach, coarsely chopped
- 2 cloves garlic, chopped
- Salt and freshly ground black pepper, to taste
- 2 tablespoons unsalted butter, divided
- 4 Sole fillets (about 680 g)
- Dash of paprika
- ½ lemon, sliced into 4 wedges

Preparation Instructions :
1. Place the pine nuts in a baking dish that fits in your air fryer. Set the air fryer to 204°C and air fry for 4 minutes until the nuts are lightly browned and fragrant. Remove the baking dish from the air fryer, tip the nuts onto a plate to cool, and continue preheating the air fryer. When the nuts are cool enough to handle, chop them into fine pieces.
2. In the baking dish, combine the oil, tomatoes, spinach, and garlic. Use tongs to toss until thoroughly combined. Air fry for 5 minutes until the tomatoes are softened and the spinach is wilted.
3. Transfer the vegetables to a bowl and stir in the toasted pine nuts. Season to taste with salt and freshly ground black pepper.
4. Place 1 tablespoon of the butter in the bottom of the baking dish. Lower the heat on the air fryer to 176°C.
5. Place the sole on a clean work surface. Sprinkle both sides with salt and black pepper. Divide the vegetable mixture among the sole fillets and carefully roll up, securing with toothpicks.
6. Working in batches if necessary, arrange the fillets seam-side down in the baking dish along with 1 tablespoon of water. Top the fillets with remaining 1 tablespoon butter and sprinkle with a dash of paprika.
7. Cover loosely with foil and air fry for 10 to 15 minutes until the fish is opaque and flakes easily with a fork. Remove the toothpicks before serving with the lemon wedges.

Friday Night Fish-Fry

Prep time: 10 minutes/ Cook time: 10 minutes/ Serves 4

Ingredients :
- 1 large egg
- 45 g powdered Parmesan cheese
- 1 teaspoon smoked paprika
- ¼ teaspoon celery salt
- ¼ teaspoon ground black pepper
- 4 cod fillets, 110 g each
- Chopped fresh oregano or parsley, for garnish (optional)
- Lemon slices, for serving (optional)

Preparation Instructions :
1. Spray the air fryer basket with avocado oil. Preheat the air fryer to 204°C.
2. Crack the egg in a shallow bowl and beat it lightly with a fork. Combine the Parmesan cheese, paprika, celery salt, and pepper in a separate shallow bowl.
3. One at a time, dip the fillets into the egg, then dredge them in the Parmesan

mixture. Using your hands, press the Parmesan onto the fillets to form a nice crust. As you finish, place the fish in the air fryer basket.
4. Air fry the fish in the air fryer for 10 minutes, or until it is cooked through and flakes easily with a fork. Garnish with fresh oregano or parsley and serve with lemon slices, if desired.
5. Store leftovers in an airtight container in the refrigerator for up to 3 days. Reheat in a preheated 204°C air fryer for 5 minutes, or until warmed through.

Salmon with Fennel and Carrot

Prep time: 15 minutes/ Cook time: 15 minutes/ Serves 4

Ingredients :
- 1 fennel bulb, thinly sliced
- 2 large carrots, sliced
- 1 large onion, thinly sliced
- 2 teaspoons extra-virgin olive oil
- 120 ml sour cream
- 1 teaspoon dried tarragon leaves
- 4 (140 g) salmon fillets
- ⅛ teaspoon salt
- ¼ teaspoon coarsely ground black pepper

Preparation Instructions :
1. Insert the crisper plate into the basket and the basket into the unit. Preheat the unit to 204°C,
2. In a medium bowl, toss together the fennel, carrots, and onion. Add the olive oil and toss again to coat the vegetables. Put the vegetables into a 6-inch round metal pan.
3. Once the unit is preheated, place the pan into the basket.
4. Cook for 15 minutes.
5. Check after 5 minutes, the vegetables should be crisp-tender. Remove the pan and stir in the sour cream and tarragon. Top with the salmon fillets and sprinkle the fish with the salt and pepper. Reinsert the pan into the basket and resume cooking.
6. When the cooking is complete, the salmon should flake easily with a fork and a food thermometer should register at least 64°C. Serve the salmon on top of the vegetables.

Mackerel with Spinach

Prep time: 15 minutes/ Cook time: 20 minutes/ Serves 5

Ingredients :
- 455 g mackerel, trimmed
- 1 bell pepper, chopped
- 15 g spinach, chopped
- 1 tablespoon avocado oil
- 1 teaspoon ground black pepper
- 1 teaspoon tomato paste

Preparation Instructions :
1. In the mixing bowl, mix bell pepper with spinach, ground black pepper, and tomato paste.
2. Fill the mackerel with spinach mixture.
3. Then brush the fish with avocado oil and put it in the air fryer.
4. Cook the fish at 185°C for 20 minutes.

Garlic Butter Prawns Scampi

Prep time: 5 minutes/ Cook time: 8 minutes/ Serves 4

Ingredients :
Sauce:
- 60 g unsalted butter
- 2 tablespoons fish stock or chicken broth

- 2 cloves garlic, minced
- 2 tablespoons chopped fresh basil leaves
- 1 tablespoon lemon juice
- 1 tablespoon chopped fresh parsley, plus more for garnish
- 1 teaspoon red pepper flakes

Prawns:
- 455 g large prawns, peeled and deveined, tails removed
- Fresh basil sprigs, for garnish

Preparation Instructions :

1. Preheat the air fryer to 176ºC.
2. Put all the ingredients for the sauce in a baking pan and stir to incorporate.
3. Transfer the baking pan to the air fryer and air fry for 3 minutes, or until the sauce is heated through.
4. Once done, add the prawns to the baking pan, flipping to coat in the sauce.
5. Return to the air fryer and cook for another 5 minutes, or until the prawns are pink and opaque. Stir the prawns twice during cooking.
6. Serve garnished with the parsley and basil sprigs.

Honey-Balsamic Salmon

Prep time: 5 minutes/ Cook time: 8 minutes/ Serves 2

Ingredients :
- Olive or vegetable oil, for spraying
- 2 (170 g) salmon fillets
- 60 ml balsamic vinegar
- 2 tablespoons honey
- 2 teaspoons red pepper flakes
- 2 teaspoons olive oil
- ½ teaspoon salt
- ¼ teaspoon freshly ground black pepper

Preparation Instructions :

1. Line the air fryer basket with baking paper and spray lightly with oil.
2. Place the salmon in the prepared basket.
3. In a small bowl, whisk together the balsamic vinegar, honey, red pepper flakes, olive oil, salt, and black pepper. Brush the mixture over the salmon.
4. Roast at 200ºC for 7 to 8 minutes, or until the internal temperature reaches 64ºC. Serve immediately.

Air Fried Crab Bun

Prep time: 15 minutes/ Cook time: 20 minutes/ Serves 2

Ingredients :
- 140 g crab meat, chopped
- 2 eggs, beaten
- 2 tablespoons coconut flour
- ¼ teaspoon baking powder
- ½ teaspoon coconut aminos, or tamari
- ½ teaspoon ground black pepper
- 1 tablespoon coconut oil, softened

Preparation Instructions :

1. In the mixing bowl, mix crab meat with eggs, coconut flour, baking powder, coconut aminos, ground black pepper, and coconut oil.
2. Knead the smooth dough and cut it into pieces.
3. Make the buns from the crab mixture and put them in the air fryer basket.
4. Cook the crab buns at 185ºC for 20 minutes.

Oregano Tilapia Fingers

Prep time: 15 minutes/ Cook time: 9 minutes/ Serves 4

Ingredients :
- 455 g tilapia fillet
- 60 g coconut flour
- 2 eggs, beaten

- ½ teaspoon ground paprika
- 1 teaspoon dried oregano
- 1 teaspoon avocado oil

Preparation Instructions :

1. Cut the tilapia fillets into fingers and sprinkle with ground paprika and dried oregano.
2. Then dip the tilapia fingers in eggs and coat in the coconut flour.
3. Sprinkle fish fingers with avocado oil and cook in the air fryer at 188°C for 9 minutes.

Salmon on Bed of Fennel and Carrot

Prep time: 15 minutes/ Cook time: 13 to 14 minutes/ Serves 2

Ingredients :

- 1 fennel bulb, thinly sliced
- 1 large carrot, peeled and sliced
- 1 small onion, thinly sliced
- 60 ml low-fat sour cream
- ¼ teaspoon coarsely ground pepper
- 2 salmon fillets, 140 g each

Preparation Instructions :

1. Combine the fennel, carrot, and onion in a bowl and toss.
2. Put the vegetable mixture into a baking pan. Roast in the air fryer at 204°C for 4 minutes or until the vegetables are crisp-tender.
3. Remove the pan from the air fryer. Stir in the sour cream and sprinkle the vegetables with the pepper.
4. Top with the salmon fillets.
5. Return the pan to the air fryer. Roast for another 9 to 10 minutes or until the salmon just barely flakes when tested with a fork.

Rainbow Salmon Kebabs

Prep time: 10 minutes/ Cook time: 8 minutes/ Serves 2

Ingredients :

- 170 g boneless, skinless salmon, cut into 1-inch cubes
- ¼ medium red onion, peeled and cut into 1-inch pieces
- ½ medium yellow bell pepper, seeded and cut into 1-inch pieces
- ½ medium courgette, trimmed and cut into ½-inch slices
- 1 tablespoon olive oil
- ½ teaspoon salt
- ¼ teaspoon ground black pepper

Preparation Instructions :

1. Using one (6-inch) skewer, skewer 1 piece salmon, then 1 piece onion, 1 piece bell pepper, and finally 1 piece courgette. Repeat this pattern with additional skewers to make four kebabs total. Drizzle with olive oil and sprinkle with salt and black pepper.
2. Place kebabs into ungreased air fryer basket. Adjust the temperature to 204°C and air fry for 8 minutes, turning kebabs halfway through cooking. Salmon will easily flake and have an internal temperature of at least 64°C when done; vegetables will be tender. Serve warm.

Prawn Kebabs

Prep time: 15 minutes/ Cook time: 6 minutes/ Serves 4

Ingredients :

- Olive or vegetable oil, for spraying
- 455 g medium raw prawns, peeled and deveined
- 4 tablespoons unsalted butter, melted

- 1 tablespoon Old Bay seasoning
- 1 tablespoon packed light brown sugar
- 1 teaspoon granulated garlic
- 1 teaspoon onion powder
- ½ teaspoon freshly ground black pepper

Preparation Instructions :

1. Line the air fryer basket with baking paper and spray lightly with oil.
2. Thread the prawns onto the skewers and place them in the prepared basket.
3. In a small bowl, mix together the butter, Old Bay, brown sugar, garlic, onion powder, and black pepper. Brush the sauce on the prawns.
4. Air fry at 204°C for 5 to 6 minutes, or until pink and firm. Serve immediately.

Smoky Prawns and Chorizo Tapas

Prep time: 15 minutes/ Cook time: 10 minutes/ Serves 2 to 4

Ingredients :

- 110 g Spanish (cured) chorizo, halved horizontally and sliced crosswise
- 230 g raw medium prawns, peeled and deveined
- 1 tablespoon extra-virgin olive oil
- 1 small shallot, halved and thinly sliced
- 1 garlic clove, minced
- 1 tablespoon finely chopped fresh oregano
- ½ teaspoon smoked Spanish paprika
- ¼ teaspoon kosher or coarse sea salt
- ¼ teaspoon black pepper
- 3 tablespoons fresh orange juice
- 1 tablespoon minced fresh parsley

Preparation Instructions :

1. Place the chorizo in a baking pan. Set the pan in the air fryer basket. Set the air fryer to 192°C for 5 minutes, or until the chorizo has started to brown and render its fat.
2. Meanwhile, in a large bowl, combine the prawns, olive oil, shallot, garlic, oregano, paprika, salt, and pepper. Toss until the prawns are well coated.
3. Transfer the prawns to the pan with the chorizo. Stir to combine. Place the pan in the air fryer basket. Cook for 10 minutes, stirring halfway through the cooking time.
4. Transfer the prawns and chorizo to a serving dish. Drizzle with the orange juice and toss to combine. Sprinkle with the parsley.

Swordfish Skewers with Caponata

Prep time: 15 minutes/ Cook time: 20 minutes/ Serves 2

Ingredients :

- 280 g small Italian aubergine, cut into 1-inch pieces
- 170 g cherry tomatoes
- 3 spring onions, cut into 2 inches long
- 2 tablespoons extra-virgin olive oil, divided
- Salt and pepper, to taste
- 340 g skinless swordfish steaks, 1¼ inches thick, cut into 1-inch pieces
- 2 teaspoons honey, divided
- 2 teaspoons ground coriander, divided
- 1 teaspoon grated lemon zest, divided
- 1 teaspoon juice
- 4 (6-inch) wooden skewers
- 1 garlic clove, minced
- ½ teaspoon ground cumin
- 1 tablespoon chopped fresh basil

Preparation Instructions :

1. Preheat the air fryer to 204°C.
2. Toss aubergine, tomatoes, and spring onions with 1 tablespoon oil, ¼ teaspoon salt, and ⅛ teaspoon pepper in bowl;

transfer to air fryer basket. Air fry until aubergine is softened and browned and tomatoes have begun to burst, about 14 minutes, tossing halfway through cooking. Transfer vegetables to cutting board and set aside to cool slightly.

3. Pat swordfish dry with paper towels. Combine 1 teaspoon oil, 1 teaspoon honey, 1 teaspoon coriander, ½ teaspoon lemon zest, ⅛ teaspoon salt, and pinch pepper in a clean bowl. Add swordfish and toss to coat. Thread swordfish onto skewers, leaving about ¼ inch between each piece (3 or 4 pieces per skewer).
4. Arrange skewers in air fryer basket, spaced evenly apart. (Skewers may overlap slightly.) Return basket to air fryer and air fry until swordfish is browned and registers 140ºF (60ºC), 6 to 8 minutes, flipping and rotating skewers halfway through cooking.
5. Meanwhile, combine remaining 2 teaspoons oil, remaining 1 teaspoon honey, remaining 1 teaspoon coriander, remaining ½ teaspoon lemon zest, lemon juice, garlic, cumin, ¼ teaspoon salt, and ⅛ teaspoon pepper in large bowl. Microwave, stirring once, until fragrant, about 30 seconds. Coarsely chop the cooked vegetables, transfer to bowl with dressing, along with any accumulated juices, and gently toss to combine. Stir in basil and season with salt and pepper to taste. Serve skewers with caponata.

Crab Cakes with Sriracha Mayonnaise

Prep time: 15 minutes/ Cook time: 10 minutes/ Serves 4

Ingredients :

Sriracha Mayonnaise:
- 230 g mayonnaise
- 1 tablespoon Sriracha
- 1½ teaspoons freshly squeezed lemon juice

Crab Cakes:
- 1 teaspoon extra-virgin olive oil
- 40 g finely diced red bell pepper
- 40 g diced onion
- 40 g diced celery
- 455 g lump crab meat
- 1 teaspoon Old Bay seasoning
- 1 egg
- 1½ teaspoons freshly squeezed lemon juice
- 200 g panko bread crumbs, divided
- Vegetable oil, for spraying

Preparation Instructions :

1. Mix the mayonnaise, Sriracha, and lemon juice in a small bowl. Place ⅔ of the mixture in a separate bowl to form the base of the crab cakes. Cover the remaining Sriracha mayonnaise and refrigerate. (This will become dipping sauce for the crab cakes once they are cooked.)
2. Heat the olive oil in a heavy-bottomed, medium skillet over medium-high heat. Add the bell pepper, onion, and celery and sauté for 3 minutes. Transfer the vegetables to the bowl with the reserved ⅔ of Sriracha mayonnaise. Mix in the crab, Old Bay seasoning, egg, and lemon juice. Add 120 g of the panko. Form the crab mixture into 8 cakes. Dredge the cakes in the remaining panko, turning to coat. Place on a baking sheet. Cover and refrigerate for at least 1 hour and up to 8 hours.
3. Preheat the air fryer to 192ºC. Spray the air fryer basket with oil. Working in batches as needed so as not to overcrowd the basket, place the chilled crab cakes in a single layer in the basket. Spray the crab cakes with oil. Bake until golden brown, 8 to 10 minutes, carefully turning

halfway through cooking. Remove to a platter and keep warm. Repeat with the remaining crab cakes as needed. Serve the crab cakes immediately with Sriracha mayonnaise dipping sauce.

Parmesan-Crusted Halibut Fillets

Prep time: 5 minutes/ Cook time: 10 minutes/ Serves 4

Ingredients :
- 2 medium-sized halibut fillets
- Dash of tabasco sauce
- 1 teaspoon curry powder
- ½ teaspoon ground coriander
- ½ teaspoon hot paprika
- 1½ tablespoons olive oil
- Kosher or coarse sea salt, and freshly cracked mixed peppercorns, to taste
- 2 eggs
- 75 g grated Parmesan cheese

Preparation Instructions :
1. Preheat the air fryer to 185°C.
2. On a clean work surface, drizzle the halibut fillets with the tabasco sauce. Sprinkle with the curry powder, coriander, hot paprika, salt, and cracked mixed peppercorns. Set aside.
3. In a shallow bowl, beat the eggs until frothy. In another shallow bowl, combine the olive oil and Parmesan cheese.
4. One at a time, dredge the halibut fillets in the beaten eggs, shaking off any excess, then roll them over the Parmesan cheese until evenly coated.
5. Arrange the halibut fillets in the air fryer basket in a single layer and air fry for 10 minutes, or until the fish is golden brown and crisp.
6. Cool for 5 minutes before serving.

Mediterranean-Style Cod

Prep time: 5 minutes/ Cook time: 12 minutes/ Serves 4

Ingredients :
- 4 cod fillets, 170 g each
- 3 tablespoons fresh lemon juice
- 1 tablespoon olive oil
- ¼ teaspoon salt
- 6 cherry tomatoes, halved
- 45 g pitted and sliced kalamata olives

Preparation Instructions :
1. Place cod into an ungreased round nonstick baking dish. Pour lemon juice into dish and drizzle cod with olive oil. Sprinkle with salt. Place tomatoes and olives around baking dish in between fillets.
2. Place dish into air fryer basket. Adjust the temperature to 176°C and bake for 12 minutes, carefully turning cod halfway through cooking. Fillets will be lightly browned, easily flake, and have an internal temperature of at least 64°C when done. Serve warm.

Simple Buttery Cod

Prep time: 5 minutes/ Cook time: 8 minutes/ Serves 2

Ingredients :
- 2 cod fillets, 110 g each
- 2 tablespoons salted butter, melted
- 1 teaspoon Old Bay seasoning
- ½ medium lemon, sliced

Preparation Instructions :
1. Place cod fillets into a round baking dish. Brush each fillet with butter and sprinkle with Old Bay seasoning. Lay two lemon slices on each fillet. Cover the dish with

foil and place into the air fryer basket.
2. Adjust the temperature to 176°C and bake for 8 minutes. Flip halfway through the cooking time. When cooked, internal temperature should be at least 64°C. Serve warm.

Classic Prawns Empanadas

Prep time: 10 minutes/ Cook time: 8 minutes/ Serves 5

Ingredients :

- 230 g raw prawns, peeled, deveined and chopped
- 1 small chopped red onion
- 1 spring onion, chopped
- 2 garlic cloves, minced
- 2 tablespoons minced red bell pepper
- 2 tablespoons chopped fresh coriander
- ½ tablespoon fresh lime juice
- ¼ teaspoon sweet paprika
- ⅛ teaspoon kosher salt
- ⅛ teaspoon crushed red pepper flakes (optional)
- 1 large egg, beaten
- 10 frozen Goya Empanada Discos, thawed
- Cooking spray

Preparation Instructions :

1. In a medium bowl, combine the prawns, red onion, spring onion, garlic, bell pepper, coriander, lime juice, paprika, salt, and pepper flakes (if using).
2. In a small bowl, beat the egg with 1 teaspoon water until smooth.
3. Place an empanada disc on a work surface and put 2 tablespoons of the prawn mixture in the center. Brush the outer edges of the disc with the egg wash. Fold the disc over and gently press the edges to seal. Use a fork and press around the edges to crimp and seal completely. Brush the tops of the empanadas with the egg wash.
4. Preheat the air fryer to 192°C.
5. Spray the bottom of the air fryer basket with cooking spray to prevent sticking. Working in batches, arrange a single layer of the empanadas in the air fryer basket and air fry for about 8 minutes, flipping halfway, until golden brown and crispy.
6. Serve hot.

Lemony Prawns

Prep time: 10 minutes/ Cook time: 7 to 8 minutes/ Serves 4

Ingredients :

- 455 g prawns, peeled and deveined
- 4 tablespoons olive oil
- 1½ tablespoons lemon juice
- 1½ tablespoons fresh parsley, roughly chopped
- 2 cloves garlic, finely minced
- 1 teaspoon crushed red pepper flakes, or more to taste
- Garlic pepper, to taste
- Sea salt flakes, to taste

Preparation Instructions :

1. Preheat the air fryer to 196°C.
2. Toss all the ingredients in a large bowl until the prawns are coated on all sides.
3. Arrange the prawns in the air fryer basket and air fry for 7 to 8 minutes, or until the prawns are pink and cooked through.
4. Serve warm.

Crustless Prawn Quiche

Prep time: 15 minutes/ Cook time: 20 minutes/ Serves 2

Ingredients :

- Vegetable oil

- 4 large eggs
- 120 ml single cream
- 110 g raw prawns, chopped
- 120 g shredded Parmesan or Swiss cheese
- 235 g chopped spring onions
- 1 teaspoon sweet smoked paprika
- 1 teaspoon Herbes de Provence
- 1 teaspoon black pepper
- ½ to 1 teaspoon kosher or coarse sea salt

Preparation Instructions :

1. Generously grease a baking pan with vegetable oil. (Be sure to grease the pan well, the proteins in eggs stick something fierce. Alternatively, line the bottom of the pan with baking paper cut to fit and spray the baking paper and sides of the pan generously with vegetable oil spray.)
2. In a large bowl, beat together the eggs and single cream. Add the prawns, 90 g of the cheese, the scallions, paprika, Herbes de Provence, pepper, and salt. Stir with a fork to thoroughly combine. Pour the egg mixture into the prepared pan.
3. Place the pan in the air fryer basket. Set the air fryer to 150°C for 20 minutes. After 17 minutes, sprinkle the remaining 30 g cheese on top and cook for the remaining 3 minutes, or until the cheese has melted, the eggs are set, and a toothpick inserted into the center comes out clean.
4. Serve the quiche warm or at room temperature.

Chapter 6 Vegetables and Sides

Garlic-Parmesan Crispy Baby Potatoes

Prep time: 10 minutes/ Cook time: 15 minutes/ Serves 4

Ingredients :

- Oil, for spraying
- 450 g baby potatoes
- 45 g grated Parmesan cheese, divided
- 3 tablespoons olive oil
- 2 teaspoons garlic powder
- ½ teaspoon onion powder
- ½ teaspoon salt
- ¼ teaspoon freshly ground black pepper
- ¼ teaspoon paprika
- 2 tablespoons chopped fresh parsley, for garnish

Preparation Instructions :

1. Line the air fryer basket with parchment and spray lightly with oil.
2. Rinse the potatoes, pat dry with paper towels, and place in a large bowl.
3. In a small bowl, mix together 45 g of Parmesan cheese, the olive oil, garlic, onion powder, salt, black pepper, and paprika. Pour the mixture over the potatoes and toss to coat.
4. Transfer the potatoes to the prepared basket and spread them out in an even layer, taking care to keep them from touching. You may need to work in batches, depending on the size of your air fryer.
5. Air fry at 200°C for 15 minutes, stirring after 7 to 8 minutes, or until easily pierced with a fork. Continue to cook for another 1 to 2 minutes, if needed.
6. Sprinkle with the parsley and the remaining Parmesan cheese and serve.

Lebanese Baba Ghanoush

Prep time: 15 minutes/ Cook time: 20 minutes/ Serves 4

Ingredients :

- 1 medium aubergine
- 2 tablespoons vegetable oil
- 2 tablespoons tahini (sesame paste)
- 2 tablespoons fresh lemon juice
- ½ teaspoon coarse sea salt
- 1 tablespoon extra-virgin olive oil
- ½ teaspoon smoked paprika
- 2 tablespoons chopped fresh parsley

Preparation Instructions :

1. Rub the aubergine all over with the vegetable oil. Place the aubergine in the air fryer basket. Set the air fryer to 200°C for 20 minutes, or until the aubergine skin is blistered and charred.
2. Transfer the aubergine to a re-sealable plastic bag, seal, and set aside for 15 minutes (the aubergine will finish cooking in the residual heat trapped in the bag).
3. Transfer the aubergine to a large bowl. Peel off and discard the charred skin. Roughly mash the aubergine flesh. Add the tahini, lemon juice, and salt. Stir to combine.
4. Transfer the mixture to a serving bowl. Drizzle with the olive oil. Sprinkle with the paprika and parsley and serve.

Parmesan-Thyme Butternut Squash

Prep time: 15 minutes/ Cook time: 20 minutes/ Serves 4

Ingredients :
- 350 g butternut squash, cubed into 1-inch pieces (approximately 1 medium)
- 2 tablespoons olive oil
- ¼ teaspoon salt
- ¼ teaspoon garlic powder
- ¼ teaspoon black pepper
- 1 tablespoon fresh thyme
- 20 g grated Parmesan

Preparation Instructions :
1. Preheat the air fryer to 180°C.
2. In a large bowl, combine the cubed squash with the olive oil, salt, garlic powder, pepper, and thyme until the squash is well coated.
3. Pour this mixture into the air fryer basket, and roast for 10 minutes. Stir and roast another 8 to 10 minutes more.
4. Remove the squash from the air fryer and toss with freshly grated Parmesan before serving.

Fried Brussels Sprouts

Prep time: 10 minutes/ Cook time: 18 minutes/ Serves 4

Ingredients :
- 1 teaspoon plus 1 tablespoon extra-virgin olive oil, divided
- 2 teaspoons minced garlic
- 2 tablespoons honey
- 1 tablespoon sugar
- 2 tablespoons freshly squeezed lemon juice
- 2 tablespoons rice vinegar
- 2 tablespoons sriracha
- 450 g Brussels sprouts, stems trimmed and any tough leaves removed, rinsed, halved lengthwise, and dried
- ½ teaspoon salt
- Cooking oil spray

Preparation Instructions :
1. In a small saucepan over low heat, combine 1 teaspoon of olive oil, the garlic, honey, sugar, lemon juice, vinegar, and sriracha. Cook for 2 to 3 minutes, or until slightly thickened. Remove the pan from the heat, cover, and set aside.
2. Place the Brussels sprouts in a resealable bag or small bowl. Add the remaining olive oil and the salt, and toss to coat.
3. Insert the crisper plate into the basket and the basket into the unit. Preheat the unit by selecting AIR FRY, setting the temperature to 200°C, and setting the time to 3 minutes. Select START/STOP to begin.
4. Once the unit is preheated, spray the crisper plate with cooking oil. Add the Brussels sprouts to the basket.
5. Select AIR FRY, set the temperature to 200°C, and set the time to 15 minutes. Select START/STOP to begin.
6. After 7 or 8 minutes, remove the basket and shake it to toss the sprouts. Reinsert the basket to resume cooking.
7. When the cooking is complete, the leaves should be crispy and light brown and the sprout centres tender.
8. Place the sprouts in a medium serving bowl and drizzle the sauce over the top. Toss to coat, and serve immediately.

Fried Courgette Salad

Prep time: 10 minutes/ Cook time: 5 to 7 minutes/ Serves 4

Ingredients :
- 2 medium courgette, thinly sliced
- 5 tablespoons olive oil, divided
- 15 g chopped fresh parsley
- 2 tablespoons chopped fresh mint
- Zest and juice of ½ lemon
- 1 clove garlic, minced
- 65 g crumbled feta cheese
- Freshly ground black pepper, to taste

Preparation Instructions :

1. Preheat the air fryer to 200°C.
2. In a large bowl, toss the courgette slices with 1 tablespoon of the olive oil.
3. Working in batches if necessary, arrange the courgette slices in an even layer in the air fryer basket. Pausing halfway through the cooking time to shake the basket, air fry for 5 to 7 minutes until soft and lightly browned on each side.
4. Meanwhile, in a small bowl, combine the remaining 4 tablespoons olive oil, parsley, mint, lemon zest, lemon juice, and garlic.
5. Arrange the courgette on a plate and drizzle with the dressing. Sprinkle the feta and black pepper on top. Serve warm or at room temperature.

Spicy Roasted Bok Choy

Prep time: 10 minutes/ Cook time: 7 to 10 minutes/ Serves 4

Ingredients :

- 2 tablespoons olive oil
- 2 tablespoons reduced-sodium coconut aminos
- 2 teaspoons sesame oil
- 2 teaspoons chili-garlic sauce
- 2 cloves garlic, minced
- 1 head (about 450 g) bok choy, sliced lengthwise into quarters
- 2 teaspoons black sesame seeds

Preparation Instructions :

1. Preheat the air fryer to 200°C.
2. In a large bowl, combine the olive oil, coconut aminos, sesame oil, chili-garlic sauce, and garlic. Add the bok choy and toss, massaging the leaves with your hands if necessary, until thoroughly coated.
3. Arrange the bok choy in the basket of the air fryer. Pausing about halfway through the cooking time to shake the basket, air fry for 7 to 10 minutes until the bok choy is tender and the tips of the leaves begin to crisp. 4. Remove from the basket and let cool for a few minutes before coarsely chopping. Serve sprinkled with the sesame seeds.

Marinara Pepperoni Mushroom Pizza

Prep time: 5 minutes/ Cook time: 18 minutes/ Serves 4

Ingredients :

- 4 large portobello mushrooms, stems removed
- 4 teaspoons olive oil
- 225 g marinara sauce
- 225 g shredded Mozzarella cheese
- 10 slices sugar-free pepperoni

Preparation Instructions :

1. Preheat the air fryer to 192°C.
2. Brush each mushroom cap with the olive oil, one teaspoon for each cap.
3. Put on a baking sheet and bake, stem-side down, for 8 minutes.
4. Take out of the air fryer and divide the marinara sauce, Mozzarella cheese and pepperoni evenly among the caps.
5. Air fry for another 10 minutes until browned.
6. Serve hot.

Fig, Chickpea, and Rocket Salad

Prep time: 15 minutes/ Cook time: 20 minutes/ Serves 4

Ingredients :

- 8 fresh figs, halved
- 250 g cooked chickpeas
- 1 teaspoon crushed roasted cumin seeds
- 4 tablespoons balsamic vinegar

- 2 tablespoons extra-virgin olive oil, plus more for greasing
- Salt and ground black pepper, to taste
- 40 g rocket, washed and dried

Preparation Instructions :

1. Preheat the air fryer to 192ºC.
2. Cover the air fryer basket with aluminum foil and grease lightly with oil. Put the figs in the air fryer basket and air fry for 10 minutes.
3. In a bowl, combine the chickpeas and cumin seeds.
4. Remove the air fried figs from the air fryer and replace with the chickpeas. Air fry for 10 minutes. Leave to cool.
5. In the meantime, prepare the dressing. Mix the balsamic vinegar, olive oil, salt and pepper.
6. In a salad bowl, combine the rocket with the cooled figs and chickpeas.
7. Toss with the sauce and serve.

Herbed Shiitake Mushrooms

Prep time: 10 minutes/ Cook time: 5 minutes/ Serves 4

Ingredients :

- 230 g shiitake mushrooms, stems removed and caps roughly chopped
- 1 tablespoon olive oil
- ½ teaspoon salt
- Freshly ground black pepper, to taste
- 1 teaspoon chopped fresh thyme leaves
- 1 teaspoon chopped fresh oregano
- 1 tablespoon chopped fresh parsley

Preparation Instructions :

1. Preheat the air fryer to 200ºC.
2. Toss the mushrooms with the olive oil, salt, pepper, thyme and oregano. Air fry for 5 minutes, shaking the basket once or twice during the cooking process. The mushrooms will still be somewhat chewy with a meaty texture. If you'd like them a little more tender, add a couple of minutes to this cooking time.
3. Once cooked, add the parsley to the mushrooms and toss. Season again to taste and serve.

Dijon Roast Cabbage

Prep time: 10 minutes/ Cook time: 10 minutes/ Serves 4

Ingredients :

- 1 small head cabbage, cored and sliced into 1-inch-thick slices
- 2 tablespoons olive oil, divided
- ½ teaspoon salt
- 1 tablespoon Dijon mustard
- 1 teaspoon apple cider vinegar
- 1 teaspoon granular erythritol

Preparation Instructions :

1. Drizzle each cabbage slice with 1 tablespoon olive oil, then sprinkle with salt. Place slices into ungreased air fryer basket, working in batches if needed. Adjust the temperature to 180ºC and air fry for 10 minutes. Cabbage will be tender and edges will begin to brown when done.
2. In a small bowl, whisk remaining olive oil with mustard, vinegar, and erythritol. Drizzle over cabbage in a large serving dish. Serve warm.

Potato with Creamy Cheese

Prep time: 5 minutes/ Cook time: 15 minutes/ Serves 2

Ingredients :

- 2 medium potatoes
- 1 teaspoon butter
- 3 tablespoons sour cream
- 1 teaspoon chives
- 1½ tablespoons grated Parmesan cheese

Preparation Instructions :

1. Preheat the air fryer to 180°C.
2. Pierce the potatoes with a fork and boil them in water until they are cooked.
3. Transfer to the air fryer and air fry for 15 minutes.
4. In the meantime, combine the sour cream, cheese and chives in a bowl. Cut the potatoes halfway to open them up and fill with the butter and sour cream mixture.
5. Serve immediately.

Buttery Green Beans

Prep time: 5 minutes/ Cook time: 8 to 10 minutes /Serves 6

Ingredients :

- 450 g green beans, trimmed
- 1 tablespoon avocado oil
- 1 teaspoon garlic powder
- Sea salt and freshly ground black pepper, to taste
- 4 tablespoons unsalted butter, melted
- 20 g freshly grated Parmesan cheese

Preparation Instructions :

1. In a large bowl, toss together the green beans, avocado oil, and garlic powder and season with salt and pepper.
2. Set the air fryer to 200°C. Arrange the green beans in a single layer in the air fryer basket. Air fry for 8 to 10 minutes, tossing halfway through.
3. Transfer the beans to a large bowl and toss with the melted butter. Top with the Parmesan cheese and serve warm.

Roasted Grape Tomatoes and Asparagus

Prep time: 5 minutes/ Cook time: 12 minutes / Serves 6

Ingredients :

- 400 g grape tomatoes
- 1 bunch asparagus, trimmed
- 2 tablespoons olive oil
- 3 garlic cloves, minced
- ½ teaspoon coarse sea salt

Preparation Instructions :

1. Preheat the air fryer to 192°C.
2. In a large bowl, combine all of the ingredients, tossing until the vegetables are well coated with oil.
3. Pour the vegetable mixture into the air fryer basket and spread into a single layer, then roast for 12 minutes.

Mexican Corn in a Cup

Prep time: 5 minutes/ Cook time: 10 minutes/ Serves 4

Ingredients :

- 650 g frozen corn kernels (do not thaw)
- Vegetable oil spray
- 2 tablespoons butter
- 60 g sour cream
- 60 g mayonnaise
- 20 g grated Parmesan cheese (or feta, cotija, or queso fresco)
- 2 tablespoons fresh lemon or lime juice
- 1 teaspoon chili powder
- Chopped fresh green onion (optional)
- Chopped fresh coriander (optional)

Preparation Instructions :

1. Place the corn in the bottom of the air fryer basket and spray with vegetable oil spray. Set the air fryer to 180°C for 10 minutes.
2. Transfer the corn to a serving bowl. Add the butter and stir until melted. Add the sour cream, mayonnaise, cheese, lemon juice, and chili powder; stir until well combined. Serve immediately with green

onion and coriander (if using).

Courgette Fritters

Prep time: 10 minutes/ Cook time: 10 minutes/ Serves 4

Ingredients :

- 2 courgette, grated (about 450 g)
- 1 teaspoon salt
- 25 g almond flour
- 20 g grated Parmesan cheese
- 1 large egg
- ¼ teaspoon dried thyme
- ¼ teaspoon ground turmeric
- ¼ teaspoon freshly ground black pepper
- 1 tablespoon olive oil
- ½ lemon, sliced into wedges

Preparation Instructions :

1. Preheat the air fryer to 200ºC. Cut a piece of parchment paper to fit slightly smaller than the bottom of the air fryer.
2. Place the courgette in a large colander and sprinkle with the salt. Let sit for 5 to 10 minutes. Squeeze as much liquid as you can from the courgette and place in a large mixing bowl. Add the almond flour, Parmesan, egg, thyme, turmeric, and black pepper. Stir gently until thoroughly combined.
3. Shape the mixture into 8 patties and arrange on the parchment paper. Brush lightly with the olive oil. Pausing halfway through the cooking time to turn the patties, air fry for 10 minutes until golden brown. Serve warm with the lemon wedges.

Lemon-Thyme Asparagus

Prep time: 5 minutes/ Cook time: 4 to 8 minutes/ Serves 4

Ingredients :

- 450 g asparagus, woody ends trimmed off
- 1 tablespoon avocado oil
- ½ teaspoon dried thyme or ½ tablespoon chopped fresh thyme
- Sea salt and freshly ground black pepper, to taste
- 60 g goat cheese, crumbled
- Zest and juice of 1 lemon
- Flaky sea salt, for serving (optional)

Preparation Instructions :

1. In a medium bowl, toss together the asparagus, avocado oil, and thyme, and season with sea salt and pepper.
2. Place the asparagus in the air fryer basket in a single layer. Set the air fryer to 200ºC and air fry for 4 to 8 minutes, to your desired doneness.
3. Transfer to a serving platter. Top with the goat cheese, lemon zest, and lemon juice. If desired, season with a pinch of flaky salt.

Five-Spice Roasted Sweet Potatoes

Prep time: 10 minutes/ Cook time: 12 minutes/ Serves 4

Ingredients :

- ½ teaspoon ground cinnamon
- ¼ teaspoon ground cumin
- ¼ teaspoon paprika
- 1 teaspoon chili powder
- ⅛ teaspoon turmeric
- ½ teaspoon salt (optional)
- Freshly ground black pepper, to taste
- 2 large sweet potatoes, peeled and cut into ¾-inch cubes
- 1 tablespoon olive oil

Preparation Instructions :

1. In a large bowl, mix together cinnamon, cumin, paprika, chili powder, turmeric, salt, and pepper to taste.
2. Add potatoes and stir well.

3. Drizzle the seasoned potatoes with the olive oil and stir until evenly coated.
4. Place seasoned potatoes in a baking pan or an ovenproof dish that fits inside your air fryer basket.
5. Cook for 6 minutes at 200°C, stop, and stir well.
6. Cook for an additional 6 minutes.

Spiced Honey-Walnut Carrots

Prep time: 5 minutes/ Cook time: 12 minutes / Serves 6

Ingredients :
- 450 g baby carrots
- 2 tablespoons olive oil
- 80 g raw honey
- ¼ teaspoon ground cinnamon
- 25 g black walnuts, chopped

Preparation Instructions :
1. Preheat the air fryer to 180°C.
2. In a large bowl, toss the baby carrots with olive oil, honey, and cinnamon until well coated.
3. Pour into the air fryer and roast for 6 minutes. Shake the basket, sprinkle the walnuts on top, and roast for 6 minutes more.
4. Remove the carrots from the air fryer and serve.

Broccoli Tots

Prep time: 15 minutes/ Cook time: 10 minutes/ Makes 24 tots

Ingredients :
- 230 g broccoli florets
- 1 egg, beaten
- ⅛ teaspoon onion powder
- ¼ teaspoon salt
- ⅛ teaspoon pepper
- 2 tablespoons grated Parmesan cheese
- 25 g panko bread crumbs
- Oil for misting

Preparation Instructions :
1. Steam broccoli for 2 minutes. Rinse in cold water, drain well, and chop finely.
2. In a large bowl, mix broccoli with all other ingredients except the oil.
3. Scoop out small portions of mixture and shape into 24 tots. Lay them on a cookie sheet or wax paper as you work.
4. Spray tots with oil and place in air fryer basket in single layer.
5. Air fry at 200°C for 5 minutes. Shake basket and spray with oil again. Cook 5 minutes longer or until browned and crispy.

Garlic and Thyme Tomatoes

Prep time: 10 minutes/ Cook time: 15 minutes/ Serves 2 to 4

Ingredients :
- 4 plum tomatoes
- 1 tablespoon olive oil
- Salt and freshly ground black pepper, to taste
- 1 clove garlic, minced
- ½ teaspoon dried thyme

Preparation Instructions :
1. Preheat the air fryer to 200°C.
2. Cut the tomatoes in half and scoop out the seeds and any pithy parts with your fingers. Place the tomatoes in a bowl and toss with the olive oil, salt, pepper, garlic and thyme.
3. Transfer the tomatoes to the air fryer, cut side up. Air fry for 15 minutes. The edges should just start to brown. Let the tomatoes cool to an edible temperature for a few minutes and then use in pastas, on top of crostini, or as an accompaniment to any poultry, meat or fish.

Chapter 7 Fast and Easy Everyday Favourites

Air Fried Broccoli

Prep time: 5 minutes/ Cook time: 6 minutes/ Serves 1

Ingredients :
- 4 egg yolks
- 60 ml butter, melted
- 475 ml coconut flour
- Salt and pepper, to taste
- 475 ml broccoli florets

Preparation Instructions :
1. Preheat the air fryer to 204°C.
2. In a bowl, whisk the egg yolks and melted butter together. Throw in the coconut flour, salt and pepper, then stir again to combine well.
3. Dip each broccoli floret into the mixture and place in the air fryer basket. Air fry for 6 minutes in batches if necessary.
4. Take care when removing them from the air fryer and serve immediately.

Cheesy Potato Patties

Prep time: 5 minutes/ Cook time: 10 minutes/ Serves 8

Ingredients :
- 900 g white potatoes
- 120 ml finely chopped spring onions
- ½ teaspoon freshly ground black pepper, or more to taste
- 1 tablespoon fine sea salt
- ½ teaspoon hot paprika
- 475 ml shredded Colby or Monterey Jack cheese
- 60 ml rapeseed oil
- 235 ml crushed crackers

Preparation Instructions :
1. Preheat the air fryer to 182°C.
2. Boil the potatoes until soft. Dry them off and peel them before mashing thoroughly, leaving no lumps.
3. Combine the mashed potatoes with spring onions, pepper, salt, paprika, and cheese. Mould the mixture into balls with your hands and press with your palm to flatten them into patties.
4. In a shallow dish, combine the rapeseed oil and crushed crackers. Coat the patties in the crumb mixture. Bake the patties for about 10 minutes, in multiple batches if necessary.
5. Serve hot.

Beef Bratwursts

Prep time: 5 minutes/ Cook time: 15 minutes/ Serves 4

Ingredients :
- 4 (85 g) beef bratwursts

Preparation Instructions :
1. Preheat the air fryer to 192°C.
2. Place the beef bratwursts in the air fryer basket and air fry for 15 minutes, turning once halfway through.
3. Serve hot.

Baked Chorizo Scotch Eggs

Prep timeBaked Chorizo Scotch Eggs

Ingredients :
- 450 g Mexican chorizo or other seasoned sausage meat
- 4 soft-boiled eggs plus 1 raw egg

- 1 tablespoon water
- 120 ml plain flour
- 235 ml panko breadcrumbs
- Cooking spray

Preparation Instructions :

1. Divide the chorizo into 4 equal portions. Flatten each portion into a disc. Place a soft-boiled egg in the centre of each disc.
2. Wrap the chorizo around the egg, encasing it completely. Place the encased eggs on a plate and chill for at least 30 minutes.
3. Preheat the air fryer to 182°C.
4. Beat the raw egg with 1 tablespoon of water. Place the flour on a small plate and the panko on a second plate. Working with 1 egg at a time, roll the encased egg in the flour, then dip it in the egg mixture. Dredge the egg in the panko and place on a plate.
5. Repeat with the remaining eggs. Spray the eggs with oil and place in the air fryer basket. Bake for 10 minutes.
6. Turn and bake for an additional 5 to 10 minutes, or until browned and crisp on all sides.
7. Serve immediately.

Crunchy Fried Okra

Prep time: 5 minutes/ Cook time: 8 to 10 minutes/ Serves 4

Ingredients :

- 235 ml self-raising yellow cornmeal (alternatively add 1 tablespoon baking powder to cornmeal)
- 1 teaspoon Italian-style seasoning
- 1 teaspoon paprika
- 1 teaspoon salt
- ½ teaspoon freshly ground black pepper
- 2 large eggs, beaten
- 475 ml okra slices
- Cooking spray

Preparation Instructions :

1. Preheat the air fryer to 204°C. Line the air fryer basket with parchment paper.
2. In a shallow bowl, whisk the cornmeal, Italian-style seasoning, paprika, salt, and pepper until blended.
3. Place the beaten eggs in a second shallow bowl. Add the okra to the beaten egg and stir to coat.
4. Add the egg and okra mixture to the cornmeal mixture and stir until coated.
5. Place the okra on the parchment and spritz it with oil. Air fry for 4 minutes.
6. Shake the basket, spritz the okra with oil, and air fry for 4 to 6 minutes more until lightly browned and crispy.
7. Serve immediately.

Buttery Sweet Potatoes

Prep time: 5 minutes/ Cook time: 10 minutes/ Serves 4

Ingredients :

- 2 tablespoons butter, melted
- 1 tablespoon light brown sugar
- 2 sweet potatoes, peeled and cut into ½-inch cubes
- Cooking spray

Preparation Instructions :

1. Preheat the air fryer to 204°C. Line the air fryer basket with parchment paper.
2. In a medium bowl, 1.r together the melted butter and brown sugar until blended. Toss the sweet potatoes in the butter mixture until coated. Place the sweet potatoes on the parchment and spritz with oil. Air fry for 5 minutes. Shake the basket, spritz the sweet potatoes with oil, and air fry for 5 minutes more until they're soft enough to

cut with a fork.
3. Serve immediately.

Indian-Style Sweet Potato Fries

Prep time: 5 minutes/ Cook time: 8 minutes/ Makes 20 fries

Ingredients :

Seasoning Mixture:
- ¾ teaspoon ground coriander
- ½ teaspoon garam masala
- ½ teaspoon garlic powder
- ½ teaspoon ground cumin
- ¼ teaspoon ground cayenne pepper

Fries:
- 2 large sweet potatoes, peeled
- 2 teaspoons olive oil

Preparation Instructions :

1. Preheat the air fryer to 204ºC.
2. In a small bowl, combine the coriander, garam masala, garlic powder, cumin, and cayenne pepper. Slice the sweet potatoes into ¼-inch-thick fries.
3. In a large bowl, toss the sliced sweet potatoes with the olive oil and the seasoning mixture.
4. Transfer the seasoned sweet potatoes to the air fryer basket and fry for 8 minutes, until crispy.
5. Serve warm.

Purple Potato Chips with Rosemary

Prep time: 10 minutes/ Cook time: 9 to 14 minutes /Serves 6

Ingredients :

- 235 ml Greek yoghurt
- 2 chipotle chillies, minced
- 2 tablespoons adobo or chipotle sauce
- 1 teaspoon paprika
- 1 tablespoon lemon juice
- 10 purple fingerling or miniature potatoes
- 1 teaspoon olive oil
- 2 teaspoons minced fresh rosemary leaves
- ⅛ teaspoon cayenne pepper
- ¼ teaspoon coarse sea salt

Preparation Instructions :

1. Preheat the air fryer to 204ºC.
2. In a medium bowl, combine the yoghurt, minced chillies, adobo sauce, paprika, and lemon juice. Mix well and refrigerate.
3. Wash the potatoes and dry them with paper towels. Slice the potatoes lengthwise, as thinly as possible. You can use a mandoline, a vegetable peeler, or a very sharp knife.
4. Combine the potato slices in a medium bowl and drizzle with the olive oil; toss to coat. Air fry the chips, in batches, in the air fryer basket, for 9 to 14 minutes. Use tongs to gently rearrange the chips halfway during cooking time.
5. Sprinkle the chips with the rosemary, cayenne pepper, and sea salt.
6. Serve with the chipotle sauce for dipping. dipping.

Scalloped Veggie Mix

Prep time: 10 minutes/ Cook time: 15 minutes/ Serves 4

Ingredients :

- 1 Yukon Gold or other small white potato, thinly sliced
- 1 small sweet potato, peeled and thinly sliced
- 1 medium carrot, thinly sliced
- 60 ml minced onion
- 3 garlic cloves, minced
- 180 ml 2 percent milk

- 2 tablespoons cornflour
- ½ teaspoon dried thyme

Preparation Instructions :
1. Preheat the air fryer to 192°C.
2. In a baking pan, layer the potato, sweet potato, carrot, onion, and garlic.
3. In a small bowl, whisk the milk, cornflour, and thyme until blended.
4. Pour the milk mixture evenly over the vegetables in the pan. Bake for 15 minutes.
5. Check the casserole—it should be golden brown on top, and the vegetables should be tender.
6. Serve immediately.

Cheesy Baked Grits

Prep time: 10 minutes/ Cook time: 12 minutes / Serves 6

Ingredients :
- 180 ml hot water
- 2 (28 g) packages instant grits
- 1 large egg, beaten
- 1 tablespoon butter, melted
- 2 cloves garlic, minced
- ½ to 1 teaspoon red pepper flakes
- 235 ml shredded Cheddar cheese or jalapeño Jack cheese

Preparation Instructions :
1. Preheat the air fryer to 204°C.
2. In a baking pan, combine the water, grits, egg, butter, garlic, and red pepper flakes. Stir until well combined.
3. Stir in the shredded cheese. Place the pan in the air fryer basket and air fry for 12 minutes, or until the grits have cooked through and a knife inserted near the centre comes out clean.
4. Let stand for 5 minutes before serving.

Traditional Queso Fundido

Prep time: 10 minutes/ Cook time: 25 minutes/ Serves 4

Ingredients :
- 110 g fresh Mexican (or Spanish if unavailable) chorizo, casings removed
- 1 medium onion, chopped
- 3 cloves garlic, minced
- 235 ml chopped tomato
- 2 jalapeños, deseeded and diced
- 2 teaspoons ground cumin
- 475 ml shredded Oaxaca or Mozzarella cheese
- 120 ml half-and-half (60 ml whole milk and 60 ml cream combined)
- Celery sticks or tortilla chips, for serving

Preparation Instructions :
1. Preheat the air fryer to 204°C.
2. In a baking pan, combine the chorizo, onion, garlic, tomato, jalapeños, and cumin. Stir to combine.
3. Place the pan in the air fryer basket. Air fry for 15 minutes, or until the sausage is cooked, stirring halfway through the cooking time to break up the sausage.
4. Add the cheese and half-and-half; stir to combine. Air fry for 10 minutes, or until the cheese has melted.
5. Serve with celery sticks or tortilla chips.

Cheesy Chilli Toast

Prep time: 5 minutes/ Cook time: 5 minutes/ Serves 1

Ingredients :
- 2 tablespoons grated Parmesan cheese
- 2 tablespoons grated Mozzarella cheese
- 2 teaspoons salted butter, at room temperature
- 10 to 15 thin slices serrano chilli or

jalapeño
- 2 slices sourdough bread
- ½ teaspoon black pepper

Preparation Instructions :
1. Preheat the air fryer to 164°C.
2. In a small bowl, stir together the Parmesan, Mozzarella, butter, and chillies.
3. Spread half the mixture onto one side of each slice of bread. Sprinkle with the pepper. Place the slices, cheese-side up, in the air fryer basket. Bake for 5 minutes, or until the cheese has melted and started to brown slightly.
4. Serve immediately.

Baked Cheese Sandwich

Prep time: 5 minutes/ Cook time: 8 minutes/ Serves 2

Ingredients :
- 2 tablespoons mayonnaise
- 4 thick slices sourdough bread
- 4 thick slices Brie cheese
- 8 slices hot capicola or prosciutto

Preparation Instructions :
1. Preheat the air fryer to 176°C.
2. Spread the mayonnaise on one side of each slice of bread.
3. Place 2 slices of bread in the air fryer basket, mayonnaise-side down.
4. Place the slices of Brie and capicola on the bread and cover with the remaining two slices of bread, mayonnaise-side up. Bake for 8 minutes, or until the cheese has melted.
5. Serve immediately.

Baked Halloumi with Greek Salsa

Prep timeBaked Halloumi with Greek Salsa

Ingredients :
Salsa:
- 1 small shallot, finely diced
- 3 garlic cloves, minced
- 2 tablespoons fresh lemon juice
- 2 tablespoons extra-virgin olive oil
- 1 teaspoon freshly cracked black pepper
- Pinch of rock salt
- 120 ml finely diced English cucumber
- 1 plum tomato, deseeded and finely diced
- 2 teaspoons chopped fresh parsley
- 1 teaspoon snipped fresh dill
- 1 teaspoon snipped fresh oregano

Cheese:
- 227 g Halloumi cheese, sliced into ½-inch-thick pieces
- 1 tablespoon extra-virgin olive oil

Preparation Instructions :
Preheat the air fryer to 192°C.

For the salsa:
Combine the shallot, garlic, lemon juice, olive oil, pepper, and salt in a medium bowl. Add the cucumber, tomato, parsley, dill, and oregano. Toss gently to combine; set aside.

For the cheese:
1. Place the cheese slices in a medium bowl. Drizzle with the olive oil. Toss gently to coat. Arrange the cheese in a single layer in the air fryer basket. Bake for 6 minutes.
2. Divide the cheese among four serving plates. Top with the salsa and serve immediately.

Air Fried Butternut Squash with Chopped Hazelnuts

Prep time: 10 minutes/ Cook time: 20 minutes/ Makes 700 ml

Ingredients :
- 2 tablespoons whole hazelnuts

- 700 ml butternut squash, peeled, deseeded, and cubed
- ¼ teaspoon rock salt
- ¼ teaspoon freshly ground black pepper
- 2 teaspoons olive oil
- Cooking spray

Preparation Instructions :

1. Preheat the air fryer to 152ºC.
2. Spritz the air fryer basket with cooking spray. Arrange the hazelnuts in the preheated air fryer. Air fry for 3 minutes or until soft.
3. Chopped the hazelnuts roughly and transfer to a small bowl. Set aside.
4. Set the air fryer temperature to 182ºC. Spritz with cooking spray.
5. Put the butternut squash in a large bowl, then sprinkle with salt and pepper and drizzle with olive oil. Toss to coat well.
6. Transfer the squash in the air fryer. Air fry for 20 minutes or until the squash is soft. Shake the basket halfway through the frying time.
7. When the frying is complete, transfer the squash onto a plate and sprinkle with chopped hazelnuts before serving.

Air Fried Tortilla Chips

Prep time: 5 minutes/ Cook time: 10 minutes/ Serves 4

Ingredients :

- 4 six-inch corn tortillas, cut in half and slice into thirds
- 1 tablespoon rapeseed oil
- ¼ teaspoon rock salt
- Cooking spray

Preparation Instructions :

1. Preheat the air fryer to 182ºC.
2. Spritz the air fryer basket with cooking spray. On a clean work surface, brush the tortilla chips with rapeseed oil, then transfer the chips in the preheated air fryer. Air fry for 10 minutes or until crunchy and lightly browned.
3. Shake the basket and sprinkle with salt halfway through the cooking time.
4. Transfer the chips onto a plate lined with paper towels. Serve immediately.

Cheesy Jalapeño Cornbread

Prep timeCheesy Jalapeño Cornbread

Ingredients :

- 160 ml cornmeal
- 80 ml plain flour
- ¾ teaspoon baking powder
- 2 tablespoons margarine, melted
- ½ teaspoon rock salt
- 1 tablespoon granulated sugar
- 180 ml whole milk
- 1 large egg, beaten
- 1 jalapeño pepper, thinly sliced
- 80 ml shredded extra mature Cheddar cheese
- Cooking spray

Preparation Instructions :

1. Preheat the air fryer to 152ºC.
2. Spritz the air fryer basket with cooking spray. Combine all the ingredients in a large bowl. Stir to mix well.
3. Pour the mixture in a baking pan. Arrange the pan in the preheated air fryer. Bake for 20 minutes or until a toothpick inserted in the centre of the bread comes out clean.
4. When the cooking is complete, remove the baking pan from the air fryer and allow the bread to cool for a few minutes before slicing to serve.

Chapter 8 Desserts

Pineapple Wontons

Prep time: 15 minutes/ Cook time: 15 to 18 minutes per batch/ Serves 5

Ingredients :
- 225 g cream cheese
- 170 g finely chopped fresh pineapple
- 20 wonton wrappers
- Cooking oil spray

Preparation Instructions :
1. In a small microwave-safe bowl, heat the cream cheese in the microwave on high power for 20 seconds to soften.
2. In a medium bowl, stir together the cream cheese and pineapple until mixed well.
3. Lay out the wonton wrappers on a work surface. A clean table or large cutting board works well.
4. Spoon 1½ teaspoons of the cream cheese mixture onto each wrapper. Be careful not to overfill.
5. Fold each wrapper diagonally across to form a triangle. Bring the 2 bottom corners up toward each other. Do not close the wrapper yet. Bring up the 2 open sides and push out any air. Squeeze the open edges together to seal.
6. Insert the crisper plate into the basket and the basket into the unit. Preheat the air fryer to 200°C.
7. Once the unit is preheated, spray the crisper plate with cooking oil. Place the wontons into the basket. You can work in batches or stack the wontons. Spray the wontons with the cooking oil.
8. Cook wontons for 10 minutes, then remove the basket, flip each wonton, and spray them with more oil. Reinsert the basket to resume cooking for 5 to 8 minutes more until the wontons are light golden brown and crisp.
9. If cooking in batches, remove the cooked wontons from the basket and repeat steps 7 and 8 for the remaining wontons.
10. When the cooking is complete, cool for 5 minutes before serving.

Cream Cheese Danish

Prep time: 20 minutes/ Cook time: 15 minutes / Serves 6

Ingredients :
- 70 g blanched finely ground almond flour
- 225 g shredded Mozzarella cheese
- 140 g full-fat cream cheese, divided
- 2 large egg yolks
- 75 g powdered sweetener, divided
- 2 teaspoons vanilla extract, divided

Preparation Instructions :
1. In a large microwave-safe bowl, add almond flour, Mozzarella, and 30 g cream cheese. Mix and then microwave for 1 minute.
2. Stir and add egg yolks to the bowl. Continue stirring until soft dough forms. Add 50 g sweetener to dough and 1 teaspoon vanilla.
3. Cut a piece of baking paper to fit your air fryer basket. Wet your hands with warm water and press out the dough into a ¼-inch-thick rectangle.
4. In a medium bowl, mix remaining cream cheese, remaining sweetener, and vanilla. Place this cream cheese mixture on the

right half of the dough rectangle. Fold over the left side of the dough and press to seal. Place into the air fryer basket.
5. Adjust the temperature to 164ºC and bake for 15 minutes.
6. After 7 minutes, flip over the Danish.
7. When done, remove the Danish from baking paper and allow to completely cool before cutting.

Almond Shortbread

Prep time: 10 minutes/ Cook time: 12 minutes/ Serves 8

Ingredients :
- 110 g unsalted butter
- 100 g granulated sugar
- 1 teaspoon pure almond extract
- 125 g plain flour

Preparation Instructions :
1. In bowl of a stand mixer fitted with the paddle attachment, beat the butter and sugar on medium speed until light and fluffy (3 to 4 minutes). Add the almond extract and beat until combined (about 30 seconds). Turn the mixer to low. Add the flour a little at a time and beat for about 2 minutes more until well-incorporated.
2. Pat the dough into an even layer in a baking pan. Place the pan in the air fryer basket. Set the air fryer to 192ºC and bake for 12 minutes.
3. Carefully remove the pan from air fryer basket. While the shortbread is still warm and soft, cut it into 8 wedges.
4. Let cool in the pan on a wire rack for 5 minutes. Remove the wedges from the pan and let cool completely on the rack before serving.

Crustless Peanut Butter Cheesecake

Prep time: 10 minutes/ Cook time: 10 minutes/ Serves 2

Ingredients :
- 110 g cream cheese, softened
- 2 tablespoons powdered sweetener
- 1 tablespoon all-natural, no-sugar-added peanut butter
- ½ teaspoon vanilla extract
- 1 large egg, whisked

Preparation Instructions :
1. In a medium bowl, mix cream cheese and sweetener until smooth. Add peanut butter and vanilla, mixing until smooth. Add egg and stir just until combined.
2. Spoon mixture into an ungreased springform pan and place into air fryer basket. Adjust the temperature to 148ºC and bake for 10 minutes. Edges will be firm, but center will be mostly set with only a small amount of jiggle when done.
3. Let pan cool at room temperature 30 minutes, cover with plastic wrap, then place into refrigerator at least 2 hours. Serve chilled.

Blackberry Peach Cobbler with Vanilla

Prep time: 10 minutes/ Cook time: 20 minutes/ Serves 4

Ingredients :
Filling:
- 170 g blackberries
- 250 g chopped peaches, cut into ½-inch thick slices
- 2 teaspoons arrowroot or cornflour
- 2 tablespoons coconut sugar

- 1 teaspoon lemon juice

Topping:
- 2 tablespoons sunflower oil
- 1 tablespoon maple syrup
- 1 teaspoon vanilla
- 3 tablespoons coconut sugar
- 40 g rolled oats
- 45 g whole-wheat pastry, or plain flour
- 1 teaspoon cinnamon
- ¼ teaspoon nutmeg
- ⅛ teaspoon sea salt

Preparation Instructions :

1. Make the Filling: 1. Combine the blackberries, peaches, arrowroot, coconut sugar, and lemon juice in a baking pan.
2. Using a rubber spatula, stir until well incorporated. Set aside. Make the Topping:
3. Preheat the air fryer to 162°C 4. Combine the oil, maple syrup, and vanilla in a mixing bowl and stir well. Whisk in the remaining ingredients.
4. Spread this mixture evenly over the filling.
5. Place the pan in the air fryer basket and bake for 20 minutes, or until the topping is crispy and golden brown. Serve warm

Pecan and Cherry Stuffed Apples

Prep time: 10 minutes/ Cook time: 20 minutes/ Serves 4

Ingredients :
- 4 apples (about 565 g)
- 40 g chopped pecans
- 50 g dried tart cherries
- 1 tablespoon melted butter
- 3 tablespoons brown sugar
- ¼ teaspoon allspice
- Pinch salt
- Ice cream, for serving

Preparation Instructions :

1. Cut off top ½ inch from each apple; reserve tops. With a melon baller, core through stem ends without breaking through the bottom. (Do not trim bases.)
2. Preheat the air fryer to 176°C. Combine pecans, cherries, butter, brown sugar, allspice, and a pinch of salt. Stuff mixture into the hollow centers of the apples. Cover with apple tops. Put in the air fryer basket, using tongs. Air fry for 20 to 25 minutes, or just until tender.
3. Serve warm with ice cream.

Pecan Brownies

Prep time: 10 minutes/ Cook time: 20 minutes / Serves 6

Ingredients :
- 50 g blanched finely ground almond flour
- 55 g powdered sweetener
- 2 tablespoons unsweetened cocoa powder
- ½ teaspoon baking powder
- 55 g unsalted butter, softened
- 1 large egg
- 35 g chopped pecans
- 40 g low-carb, sugar-free chocolate chips

Preparation Instructions :

1. In a large bowl, mix almond flour, sweetener, cocoa powder, and baking powder. Stir in butter and egg.
2. Fold in pecans and chocolate chips. Scoop mixture into a round baking pan. Place pan into the air fryer basket.
3. Adjust the temperature to 148°C and bake for 20 minutes.
4. When fully cooked a toothpick inserted in center will come out clean. Allow 20

minutes to fully cool and firm up.

Baked Brazilian Pineapple

Prep time: 10 minutes/ Cook time: 10 minutes/ Serves 4

Ingredients :
- 95 g brown sugar
- 2 teaspoons ground cinnamon
- 1 small pineapple, peeled, cored, and cut into spears
- 3 tablespoons unsalted butter, melted

Preparation Instructions :
1. In a small bowl, mix the brown sugar and cinnamon until thoroughly combined.
2. Brush the pineapple spears with the melted butter. Sprinkle the cinnamon-sugar over the spears, pressing lightly to ensure it adheres well.
3. Place the spears in the air fryer basket in a single layer. (Depending on the size of your air fryer, you may have to do this in batches.) Set the air fryer to 204°C and cook for 10 minutes for the first batch (6 to 8 minutes for the next batch, as the fryer will be preheated). Halfway through the cooking time, brush the spears with butter.
4. The pineapple spears are done when they are heated through, and the sugar is bubbling. Serve hot.

Cardamom Custard

Prep time: 10 minutes/ Cook time: 25 minutes/ Serves 2

Ingredients :
- 240 ml whole milk
- 1 large egg
- 2 tablespoons granulated sugar, plus 1 teaspoon
- ¼ teaspoon vanilla bean paste or pure vanilla extract
- ¼ teaspoon ground cardamom, plus more for sprinkling

Preparation Instructions :
1. In a medium bowl, beat together the milk, egg, sugar, vanilla, and cardamom.
2. Place two ramekins in the air fryer basket. Divide the mixture between the ramekins. Sprinkle lightly with cardamom. Cover each ramekin tightly with aluminum foil. Set the air fryer to 176°C and cook for 25 minutes, or until a toothpick inserted in the center comes out clean.
3. Let the custards cool on a wire rack for 5 to 10 minutes.
4. Serve warm or refrigerate until cold and serve chilled.

Fried Cheesecake Bites

Prep time: 30 minutes/ Cook time: 2 minutes/ Makes 16 bites

Ingredients :
- 225 g cream cheese, softened
- 50 g powdered sweetener, plus 2 tablespoons, divided
- 4 tablespoons heavy cream, divided
- ½ teaspoon vanilla extract
- 50 g almond flour

Preparation Instructions :
1. In a stand mixer fitted with a paddle attachment, beat the cream cheese, 50 g of the sweetener, 2 tablespoons of the heavy cream, and the vanilla until smooth. Using a small ice-cream scoop, divide the mixture into 16 balls and arrange them on a rimmed baking sheet lined with baking paper. Freeze for 45 minutes until firm.
2. Line the air fryer basket with baking

paper and preheat the air fryer to 176ºC.
3. In a small shallow bowl, combine the almond flour with the remaining 2 tablespoons of sweetener.
4. In another small shallow bowl, place the remaining 2 tablespoons cream.
5. One at a time, dip the frozen cheesecake balls into the cream and then roll in the almond flour mixture, pressing lightly to form an even coating. Arrange the balls in a single layer in the air fryer basket, leaving room between them. Air fry for 2 minutes until the coating is lightly browned.

Chocolate and Rum Cupcakes

Prep time: 5 minutes/ Cook time: 15 minutes / Serves 6

Ingredients :
- 150 g granulated sweetener
- 140 g almond flour
- 1 teaspoon unsweetened baking powder
- 3 teaspoons cocoa powder
- ½ teaspoon baking soda
- ½ teaspoon ground cinnamon
- ¼ teaspoon grated nutmeg
- ⅛ teaspoon salt
- 120 ml milk
- 110 g butter, at room temperature
- 3 eggs, whisked
- 1 teaspoon pure rum extract
- 70 g blueberries
- Cooking spray

Preparation Instructions :
1. Preheat the air fryer to 176ºC. Spray a 6-cup muffin tin with cooking spray.
2. In a mixing bowl, combine the sweetener, almond flour, baking powder, cocoa powder, baking soda, cinnamon, nutmeg, and salt and stir until well blended.
3. In another mixing bowl, mix together the milk, butter, egg, and rum extract until thoroughly combined. Slowly and carefully pour this mixture into the bowl of dry mixture. Stir in the blueberries.
4. Spoon the batter into the greased muffin cups, filling each about three-quarters full.
5. Bake for 15 minutes, or until the center is springy and a toothpick inserted in the middle comes out clean.
6. Remove from the basket and place on a wire rack to cool. Serve immediately.

Tortilla Fried Hand Pies

Prep time: 10 minutes/ Cook time: 5 minutes per batch/ Makes 12 pies

Ingredients :
- 12 small flour tortillas (4-inch diameter)
- 160 g fig jam
- 20 g slivered almonds
- 2 tablespoons desiccated, unsweetened coconut
- Coconut, or avocado oil for misting or cooking spray

Preparation Instructions :
1. Wrap refrigerated tortillas in damp paper towels and heat in microwave 30 seconds to warm.
2. Working with one tortilla at a time, place 2 teaspoons fig jam, 1 teaspoon slivered almonds, and ½ teaspoon coconut in the center of each.
3. Moisten outer edges of tortilla all around.
4. Fold one side of tortilla over filling, to make a half-moon shape, and press down lightly on center. Using the tines of a fork, press down firmly on edges of tortilla to seal in filling.
5. Mist both sides with oil or cooking spray.

6. Place hand pies in air fryer basket, close, but not overlapping. It's fine to lean some against the sides and corners of the basket. You may need to cook in 2 batches.
7. Air fry at 200°C for 5 minutes, or until lightly browned. Serve hot.
8. Refrigerate any leftover pies in a closed container. To serve later, toss them back in the air fryer basket and cook for 2 to 3 minutes to reheat.

Eggless Farina Cake

Prep time: 30 minutes/ Cook time: 25 minutes / Serves 6

Ingredients :
- Vegetable oil
- 470 ml hot water
- 165 g chopped dried fruit, such as apricots, golden raisins, figs, and/or dates
- 165 g very fine semolina
- 235 ml milk
- 200 g granulated sugar
- 55 g ghee, butter or coconut oil, melted
- 2 tablespoons plain Greek yogurt, or sour cream
- 1 teaspoon ground cardamom
- 1 teaspoon baking powder
- ½ teaspoon baking soda
- Whipped cream, for serving

Preparation Instructions :
1. Grease a baking pan with vegetable oil.
2. In a small bowl, combine the hot water and dried fruit; set aside for 20 minutes to plump up the fruit.
3. Meanwhile, in a large bowl, whisk together the semolina, milk, sugar, ghee, yogurt and cardamom. Let stand for 20 minutes to allow the semolina to soften and absorb some of the liquid.
4. Drain the dried fruit, and gently stir it into the batter. Add the baking powder and baking soda and stir until thoroughly combined.
5. Pour the batter into the prepared pan. Set the pan in the air fryer basket. Set the air fryer to 164°C, and cook for 25 minutes, or until a toothpick inserted into the center of the cake comes out clean.
6. Let the cake cool in the pan on a wire rack for 10 minutes. Remove the cake from the pan and let cool on the rack for 20 minutes before slicing.
7. Slice and serve topped with whipped cream.

White Chocolate Cookies

Prep time: 5 minutes/ Cook time: 11 minutes/ Serves 10

Ingredients :
- 225 g unsweetened white chocolate
- 2 eggs, well beaten
- 170 g butter, at room temperature
- 185 g almond flour
- 55 g coconut flour
- 150 g granulated sweetener
- 2 tablespoons coconut oil
- ⅓ teaspoon grated nutmeg
- ⅓ teaspoon ground allspice
- ⅓ teaspoon ground anise star
- ¼ teaspoon fine sea salt

Preparation Instructions :
1. Preheat the air fryer to 176°C. Line the air fryer basket with baking paper.
2. Combine all the ingredients in a mixing bowl and knead for about 3 to 4 minutes, or until a soft dough forms. Transfer to the refrigerator to chill for 20 minutes.
3. Make the cookies: Roll the dough into 1-inch balls and transfer to baking paper-lined basket, spacing 2 inches apart.

Flatten each with the back of a spoon.
4. Bake for about 11 minutes until the cookies are golden and firm to the touch.
5. Transfer to a wire rack and let the cookies cool completely. Serve immediately.

Apple Wedges with Apricots

Prep time: 5 minutes/ Cook time: 15 to 18 minutes/ Serves 4

Ingredients :
- 4 large apples, peeled and sliced into 8 wedges
- 2 tablespoons light olive oil
- 95 g dried apricots, chopped
- 1 to 2 tablespoons granulated sugar
- ½ teaspoon ground cinnamon

Preparation Instructions :
1. Preheat the air fryer to 180ºC.
2. Toss the apple wedges with the olive oil in a mixing bowl until well coated.
3. Place the apple wedges in the air fryer basket and air fry for 12 to 15 minutes.
4. Sprinkle with the dried apricots and air fry for another 3 minutes.
5. Meanwhile, thoroughly combine the sugar and cinnamon in a small bowl.
6. Remove the apple wedges from the basket to a plate. Serve sprinkled with the sugar mixture.